Suelen da Silva Webber

Law and Philosophy

Suelen da Silva Webber

Law and Philosophy

Judicial (ir)responsibility in Heideggerian hermeneutics

ScienciaScripts

Imprint

Any brand names and product names mentioned in this book are subject to trademark, brand or patent protection and are trademarks or registered trademarks of their respective holders. The use of brand names, product names, common names, trade names, product descriptions etc. even without a particular marking in this work is in no way to be construed to mean that such names may be regarded as unrestricted in respect of trademark and brand protection legislation and could thus be used by anyone.

Cover image: www.ingimage.com

This book is a translation from the original published under ISBN 978-3-330-75476-8.

Publisher:
Sciencia Scripts
is a trademark of
Dodo Books Indian Ocean Ltd. and OmniScriptum S.R.L publishing group

120 High Road, East Finchley, London, N2 9ED, United Kingdom
Str. Armeneasca 28/1, office 1, Chisinau MD-2012, Republic of Moldova, Europe
Printed at: see last page
ISBN: 978-620-8-05035-1

"to exist means to
philosophize"

Martin Heidegger
Introduction to Philosophy

INDICE

PREFACE

I was very happy and honored to be invited to preface Dr. Suelen Webber's work. There are two reasons for this. The first is the deep admiration I have for her and her academic career. A disciple of the great professor Leonel Rocha in the study of Social Systems Theory, she wrote a book that I consider fundamental for a systematic analysis of health law in the jurisdictional field, *Decision, Risk and Health: the paradox of judicial decision in the face of requests for experimental medicines*, a theme that she consolidated in indelible letters in her brilliant doctoral thesis*: "Judicial Decision, Expectations and Social Stabilization: Rethinking Legitimation through Procedure in a Complex Society"*. The second lies in the theme that the author explores in this book, namely philosophical hermeneutics and judicial decisions, a subject that has interested me ever since I joined the federal judiciary almost 30 years ago, under the inspiration of Professor Lenio Streck, with whom I first learned about hermeneutics in 1989, during a specialization course in Civil Procedure at UFSC.

One might wonder about the compatibility between N. Luhmann's Social Systems Theory, which is at the center of Dr. Suelen Webber's studies, and Heidegger's Hermeneutic Phenomenology, a theme developed in this work. The systematic perspective in the field of interpretation presents an insurmountable aporia. The cult of the structure instead of the subject and its appearances is still so wide that it prevents a bridge from being built between Hermeneutic Phenomenology and Systems Theory, purists would say. And I hasten to reply that, although it is necessary to overcome prejudices, this is no defense.

Dr. Suelen Webber and I were students of two great thinkers of contemporary law, one a student of Systems Theory (Leonel Rocha) and the other of Philosophical Hermeneutics (Lenio Streck), as well as others who move seamlessly between the two, making invaluable contributions to the science of law.

I've become an adherent of a more eclectic stance, tinged with the attempt to bring the various systems together, a path that contemporary philosophy is taking. As I see it, before being an impediment to communicating convergent elements of both theories, they both represent epistemological options that can offer solutions to difficult cases. What would Philosophical Hermeneutics be without Systems Theory and the other way around! Or let's forget Habermas's contribution to dispelling judicial solipsism and responding more rationally to the law-morality dichotomy, which was supported by Dworkin, in his irrefutable integralism based on the cogent force of principles. Or are we going to ignore the fact that there are more convergences than divergences between the thoughts of Habermas and Gadamer, as Paul Ricouer has shown and Lenio Streck himself accepts.

Neither Hermeneutics, Criticism nor Systemic Theory should abandon the proper character of their claims, but rather take advantage of the reciprocal capacities to describe the reconstitution structures of disturbed communication, showing the human sciences that their subjective domain is pre-structured by tradition and that they themselves occupy a determined historical place, as well as to unveil this disturbed context, accusing the pathologies and pointing towards an ideal future context.

Dr. Suelen Weber's research, in this period of history marked by unprecedented judicialization, represents a new impetus to critically rethink the fundamental role of philosophy (in law) and legal interpretation, especially in the field of judicial decisions, the qualified object of hermeneutics. After all, "if philosophy already resides in our "being-there" as such, even if it is shackled and intricate, as Hidegger said, we need to free it. And this can only happen, i.e. philosophy becoming free in us, if we have mastered the pre-understanding of what it means.

This is the first contribution of this work.

Despite the advances made by Hermeneutic Phenomenology, especially since the beginning of the last century, with the generous contributions made by philosophers such as Husserl, Wittgenstein, Heidegger and Gadamer, denoting a theoretical advance that reveals a significant maturing of the process of understanding human knowledge, all this laborious phenomenological conception built up by these philosophers still lacks greater empirical operability in the field of judicial decisions. It needs to become more practical in the interpretation of judicial decisions. In other words, it needs to definitively overcome the metaphysical dualisms that still prevail in the field of interpreting the law applied by the courts.

It is essential that Hermeneutic Phenomenology, genetically well conceived, profound in its constructions, revolutionary in its way of looking at the interpretative/applicative phenomenon of Law and, above all, not very objective or, at least, rationally contestable, crosses the gates of academia, to use an expression from the legal jargon, and enters the socially sensitive, practical world. This is the great challenge facing both academia and the legal system. This is perhaps the greatest challenge of this book.

Our author delves into three seminal issues for the judiciary: the hermeneutic irresponsibility of the judge for his decisions, the quality of the reasoning behind decisions, and the techniques of judging according to other decisions already made.

Certainly, what positivist judges have been lacking is an escape from impersonality by taking responsibility for their decisions, in the author's words, a re-encounter with authenticity (The authentic way of being opens the way to new meanings) and the overcoming of pre-understandings. Above all, says our author, the judge needs to plan the arguments he intends to use in the decision and how to justify them. To do this, however, they first need to understand their way of being, their power-to-be, but they also need language.

Language is what gives order to the world. Heidegger, paraphrasing W.

von Humboldt, said that language "is what enables man to be the living being that he is as man. As the one who speaks, man is: man". Language is found everywhere. It is therefore not surprising that, as soon as man gets an idea of what is around him, he immediately encounters language too, in order to determine it in a perspective consistent with what is shown from it.

In his seminal work, *Truth and Method,* Gadamer undertakes a philosophical crusade in order to offer, in a broad sense, a re-reading of the nature of human understanding. He places language at the service of his philosophical quest for better understanding and, based on Martin Heidegger's phenomenology, expresses himself in the movement called the second linguistic turn, the hermeneutic turn or the pragmatic-linguistic turn, a philosophical movement that has profoundly marked contemporary culture, showing modern thinkers a new theory of knowledge aimed at understanding the individual in the world, in other words, the process of knowledge in its intersubjectivity.

Escaping from the closed circle of pre-understandings, preconceptions or prejudices is the philosophical dilemma that Heidegger sought to solve. The first, permanent and final task of interpretation is not to receive in advance, by means of a happy idea or popular concepts, either the previous position or the previous vision, but to ensure the scientific theme in the elaboration of these concepts from the thing itself.

Every correct interpretation has to protect itself against the arbitrariness of the occurrence of happy ideas and the limitation of the imperceptible habits of thinking, and the prerequisite for escaping these prejudices requires the being-being to direct its sights towards the thing itself. Allowing oneself to be determined by the thing itself is not a heroic task undertaken once and for all, but truly the first, constant and ultimate task. Understandings and senses are perfected (abandoned, revised and recreated) when the agent of knowledge penetrates body and soul into the meaning of the thing to be known, gets rid of prejudices until he finds a unity of meaning. It is this constant re-projecting that constitutes Heidegger's so-called hermeneutic circle.

It must not be forgotten that in the so-called ontological-linguistic turn, being is not an entity. In other words, when we talk about the norm that emerges from the text, we are not talking about a hermeneutic-interpretative process carried out in parts (along the lines of classical hermeneutics - first I know, then I interpret, and finally I apply). You don't first interpret the text and then "attach" the respective "norm". It is not a "layer of meaning" that exists apart from the text. On the contrary, when the subject encounters the text, he already emerges normed, from his condition of being-in-the-world. This operation occurs because of the ontological difference. It makes the difference. That's why, says Lenio Streck, it's impossible to deny translation, facticity and historicity, in which the fusion of horizons is the condition for the possibility of this "normation".

The infinite in Heidegger is the absence of the dominance of reason, in other words, the individual is not only rationality, but also feeling, a characteristic that makes the subject become subject by being immersed in a world. World is understood here as everything that expresses itself in the ontic, all intellectual experiences, or rather, the openness of Dasein.

Understanding will then be the possibility of interpreting from the particularity of worlds. Dasein's actual world will influence interpretation. The Heideggerian transcendental element, however, is no longer the element of the Kantian "I think", which accompanies all our statements. It is an element that precisely replaces the consciousness that is present in Kantian perception, putting in its place Dasein itself as being-there, as the there where there is veiling and unveiling, from where the question of truth arises.

The Heideggerian concept of "practical world", which is close to the concept of ai, corresponds to the context in which we move, where we arrange ourselves, where we deal with things. It is precisely this kind of concept of the practical world that is directly and fundamentally linked to the concept of truth. Gadamer welcomes the concept of facticity, but abandons transcendentality, along the lines of existential analysis, in order to develop, along more Husserlian lines, understanding in the context of a project that seeks to recover the historicity of culture and the lived world.

The interpreter is inserted and involved in a story and within it is stripped of all control. Man is more for history than history is for man. The interpreter is not a blank book, he doesn't start from zero, from a blind spot of understanding or assigning meaning, since language, like history, has a weight, a force that drives and drags him. This means that time is not an obstacle to understanding the past, but rather the environment in which authentic understanding takes place, insofar as when time and translation are absent, the key to understanding disappears.

Understanding always implies a pre-understanding which is prefigured by the interpreter's life tradition and which shapes their preconceptions. Thus, every encounter means the "suspension" of preconceptions, whether it's an encounter with a person with whom one learns about one's own nature and limits, or with a work of art or even a text.

Philosophical phenomenology represents a critical response to the tendency to escape from factuality in the understanding of the worldview, a challenge that inspired Wittgenstein, Heidegger and Gadamer in their quest to overcome the metaphysical rationality of the Kantian matrix that permeated modernity, limiting the understanding of the legal phenomenon to a subject-object relationship, a knowing subject-known object, responsible for the justification of things.

In general, judicial decisions move between trusting in the exhaustive capacity of positive law and granting the interpreter a supposed discretionary power, a solipsistic subjectivism that can only be explained by the philosophy of consciousness.

In this work we will find a philosophical reference point that allows the judge to escape from these cardinal sins of classical hermeneutics: (1) positivist dogmatism; (2) attachment to the metaphysical subject-object relationship and (3) the escape from facticity (being-being in the world).

Well, rather than being presented, the text needs to be read. So let's try to understand what it's trying to tell us. Happy reading.

Paulo Afonso Brum Vaz

Federal Judge of the TRF4 and Doctor of Laws (Unisinos)

PRESENTATION

WHAT IS RESPONSIBLE JUDGMENT?

Antoine de Saint-Exupery, in his classic work *"The Little Prince"*, has an interesting dialogue in which the king of a certain planet, who rules over everything, upon hearing the little prince's request, determines that sunset should occur at around 7:40!

From the successive crises experienced by the Brazilian state, we are moving towards a twilight of the authority of the Constitution, so that the independence of the Judiciary (and the Public Prosecutor's Office) appears to be a condition of possibility for its effective realization in the practical world. For this to happen, the legitimacy of the decision must be built on the basis of a process characterized by democracy, i.e. that those possibly affected have the opportunity to speak out and that their arguments are taken seriously.

The meeting point between Law and Literature, based on Exupery's work, lies precisely in the conditions of possibility for a democratic legal decision, especially in the sphere of judicial decision-making, in the face of the hermeneutic responsibility[1] underlying the realization of fundamental rights within the horizon of the democratic rule of law. Deciding responsibly means observing duties of care or concern for the most vulnerable members of a community, who benefit most from an environment characterized by mutual respect and recognition. Rights pre-exist the judicial decision and therefore do not depend on the discretion of the judge (Dworkin).

In the current stage of history, democracy is not limited to the electoral process or the will of the majority, due to the shift of the pole of tension of

---

[1] Responsibility "is part of a moral epistemology, and is associated with coherence, integrity and hermeneutic *accountability*, which derive from the guarantee of the foundation of democratic legal decision-making", so that the "antithesis of responsibility is political or judicial decisionism, through the weakening of the autonomy of Law as a function of Politics (...)". LIMA, Vinicius de Melo. *The Hermeneutic Theory of Decisional Responsibility. Social Rights between Judicial Activism and Democratic Legal Decision.* Curitiba: Jurua, 2016, p. 106.

social demands to the Judiciary, which requires a plural hermeneutics that has as an unavoidable presupposition the "fusion of horizons" (Gadamer) between the different perspectives that the resolution of the specific case may involve. This is because interpreters are not automatic beings, but rather participants in the construction of democratic legal decision-making, which has a basic dimension of a philosophical nature, in the light of the ethical framework based on the authenticity of being and care (Heidegger).

In this context, for a proper understanding of the phenomenon of judicial decision-making, the work of Jurist and Professor Suelen da Silva Weber, entitled "*LAW AND PHILOSOPHY: Judicial (ir)responsibility in Heideggerian hermeneutics*", which I am honored to present to the reader, is indispensable.

The book is structured in three chapters, in which the author defends authenticity and responsibility in the act of judging, since the judge cannot say "anything about anything", as Lenio Streck warns in his Critica Hermeneutica do Direito.

In a fragmented world, in which society has "stopped questioning itself" (Castoriadis), characterized by the compartmentalization of law teaching, which is reflected in legal careers, Suelen seeks to give direction to the anguish of concern for the authenticity of judicial decision-making. The "being-with" (Heidegger) and the (ab)use of precedents and summaries cannot obfuscate the duty of analytical reasoning in the specific case, paying attention to the dynamic contradiction, in consonance with the guarantee of influence and non-surprise in the construction of the "judicial-decisional solution" (Castanheira Neves).

The "blind spot" in the process, whether civil or criminal, demands that the interpreter-being (judge) be open to hermeneutic dialogue with the parties, in a duty of collaboration that has the idea of care as its philosophical foundation, as well as a (necessary) critique of the problem of judicial decisionism, which is done masterfully by the author.

And here I can testify to the efforts of Professor Suelen, with whom I had the opportunity to spend time during my PhD in Law at the University of Vale do Rio dos Sinos - UNISINOS, to contribute to the scientific debate and the improvement of judicial practices, based on her theoretical production and her worldly experience.

I congratulate the author on her academic consistency and the relevance of her work to national legal literature, and hope that the study presented here will bear fruit in the hands of the reading public.

Excellent reading, everyone!

Torres, January 2016.

Vinicius de Melo Lima, PhD in Law from UNISINOS. Master of Laws from the University of Lisbon. University Professor and Prosecutor of Justice/RS.

Initial considerations

How does a judge reach a decision? Can we control the content of court decisions in advance? Why should we comply with a court decision? These questions - and many others along these lines - have always been part of my research. It seems to me that in a democracy, in a country where almost every everyday issue, whether banal or not, is brought before the judiciary for a decision, these are questions that should resonate in everyone's mind. From our point of view, there is no single way of satisfactorily answering a question, much less just one way of observing a communication.

In our books, and in most of our previous articles, our observation started from a systematic basis. Therefore, as good systemicists, we know that observation contains several blind spots, and that although we can't eliminate them, the ideal is to always try to have an observation that keeps as many "sides of the story", sources, references or perspectives as possible. In this way, it seems to us that observing our old questions about other optics, such as philosophy, is imperative at the moment. Martin Heidegger's philosophy presents itself as an excellent reference for this incursion, not least because of the reflection of his work in Luhmannian theory.

Well, to find out how Dasein's inauthentic way of being affects judges and their hermeneutic responsibilities when making decisions. This is the central aim of this book. This theme takes on relevance from the moment it is necessary to verify how judges, in their different guises (conciliators, lay judges, judges, magistrates, justices, ministers) have made their decisions, because, in the Democratic State of Law, this is a situation that affects all citizens.

This focus arises from the moment we realize that, in a democracy, we need something other than authority to motivate compliance with a judicial decision. This is important because, if we abandon this "motivation" and rely solely on authoritarian legitimacy, we will be little different from a dictatorship. In dictatorship, in fact, there is no need for justifications or motivations, you effectively comply because the authority has ordered you to comply.

However, when we look at the decisions handed down by the judiciary in today's society, many of them lack adequate reasoning, several lack a constitutional basis, and several even lack reasoning. Most of the time, what has been called justification is an "argumentative" basis based on repeating other court decisions, ministerial opinions or simply the final word of the decision, without justification. In other words, judges are comfortable. This convenience will be observed here from a philosophical point of view, hermeneutically, as inauthenticity. The inauthenticity that makes the "us", the *das Man,* take precedence over authentic Dasein, enabling decisions to be made without unveiling meaning.

As soon as decisions are made based on this inauthentic way of being, the problem arises of the irresponsibility of the judge in relation to the case that he was legitimized to solve and, therefore, had the obligation to understand and interpret authentically. It is true that there is no zero degree of meaning, much less what we are trying to say here. However, the mere repetition of rulings or the use of motu proprio as a way of - falsely - explaining meaning is even more damaging. An authentic decision-maker will not create his arguments out of thin air, but will be allowed to understand the peculiarities of that particular case; an inauthentic one, on the other hand, will care little about this, and will decide in a metaphysical way. This costs democracy dearly and corrupts the law.

In order to observe these issues, it must be clear that the foundations of different theories cannot be mixed to the point where they lose their meaning. Therefore, Philosophy, Sociology and Law only talk about what they can talk about, without mixing.

This book, which is based on Heidegger's philosophy, is structured in three parts. In the first, *Notes on the relevance of Being and Time in analyzing the role of the judge,* in view of the density and transformative nature of Heidegger's thought, space was devoted to explaining some elements of this theory that play an essential role in the new observation proposed here. More than that, we have tried to point out how this theory is extremely closely linked to law, and how it is not possible for jurists to ignore its revolutions and evolutions.

In the second section, entitled *How inauthenticity can give rise to the camouflage of metaphysics in the decision-making process: the necessary rescue by anguish,* after clarifying the basic assumptions of Heideggerian thought, the focus was specifically on (in)authenticity as a mode of Dasein and, therefore, also of the judge, as well as the (ir)responsibilities of this decision-maker. To this end, arguments were presented to justify why judges should not allow themselves to fall into inauthenticity when deciding, unlike when they are living their daily lives. As a judge, there are responsibilities that must be assumed, and these responsibilities can only be achieved through authenticity. In this vein, it is appropriate to ask: is there still room for metaphysics in law? This chapter also deals with this.

Finally, in *How judging on the basis of other decisions masks metaphysics and costs constitutional jurisdiction dearly: between judicial (in)authenticity and (ir)responsibility,* based on all the considerations and conceptualizations made above, we began to confront some judicial decisions which, on the basis of this observation, make no sense, precisely because they were handed down by judges who were living in "us", inauthenticity, and therefore irresponsibility. What's more, we observed how the legal system itself has absurdly legitimized this type of attitude, creating statements that purport to cover all the facts, such as the Sumulas that "authorize" the judge to "pass on to the next level of jurisdiction" the responsibility for truly deciding a given case. The obstacle encountered is then seen as an absence of meaning, which poses huge problems when we talk about a democratic country in which people can no longer find answers to the question: "Why should I comply with a court decision?".

Within this scenario, in order to complement our already consolidated observations and broaden our perception of blind spots, we invite you to take a look at judicial decision-making from different perspectives. So let's see what this observation, which blends theories of philosophy and law - without forgetting our roots - has in store for us. Join us on this journey!

CHAPTER I

Notes on the relevance of *Being and Time* in analyzing the role of the judge

Addressing a topic such as the responsibility of judges in relation to the judicial decisions they make - a latent issue today - requires qualified observation. So that we are not limited to the extreme by blind spots[2]the effort is directed towards observing the problem from the most different perspectives, from various theories, seeking to introduce new angles, adding different and daring confrontations in this communication. However, without incurring in heresies such as theoretical mix-ups, in which "researchers" only use excerpts that interest them from a given theoretical matrix, and collate other authors without the slightest compatibility, producing meaningless doctrinal frauds.

At this time in history, when the Brazilian Judiciary is gaining so much prominence in society, it is necessary to analyze, within this context, the responsibilities of this judge and his conduct in this scenario. Today, practically all of life's issues are decided, await a judicial decision or are influenced by the decisions of judges at the most different levels. Judges have

---

[2] Blind spots are not good or bad in themselves, they just exist. The blind spot is something that marks and allows observation. You can't see everything. Let's look at examples: "When we have to go to the ophthalmologist. This professional examines exactly what we can't see in our eye, which is exactly what enables us to see. It's a fact that, even looking through a mirror, you can't see the whole of your own eye. The curious thing is that the ophthalmologist, in this role, can see his patient's blind spot. However, he himself cannot see his own eye, his own blind spot. The same happens with psychiatric professionals who follow a Freudian line. The patient lies down and talks about their problems, starting at any point they like, sometimes with a simple sentence. The patient can't see the problem in that situation, there's a space that he's not allowed to observe, but for a second-order observer, in this case, it's possible to see this blind spot." WEBBER, Suelen da Silva. Decision, risk and health: the paradox of judicial decision in the face of requests for experimental medicines. Curitiba: Jurua, 2013. p. 87.

therefore come to play a central role in major social issues and communications.

To begin our discussion, we need to contextualize and delimit the borders of our painting. The point we want to observe here is the moment when a judicial decision is made, not with the intention of dogmatically stating the steps for making a decision, or with the intention of demonstrating a way to anticipate and control the content of judicial decisions, limiting it, much less do we want to arrive at a correct answer. Our aim is to observe how some forms of decision-making completely ignore philosophical findings and thereby affect social dynamics. You see, on this hermeneutic basis, we can say that the concern with judgment is not focused on which law will be applied, but on a previous instance, which lies in authenticity and responsibility. Thus, our place of observation will necessarily be in the writings of Martin Heidegger.

It is therefore essential that the analysis intended here starts its argument from the most basic assumptions of the theory developed by Heidegger. This sophisticated observation will deal with (ir)responsibility and anguish, not in their traditional conceptions, but from a philosophical perspective, which finds its basis in Heideggerian thought.

Heidegger's thought is one of the most important of the 20th century, and has entered the 21st century with unparalleled relevance and timeliness. In fact, thinking only in the field of philosophy - if such a "split" is possible - Heidegger is probably one of the most important philosophers of all time. So let's start with the factual context of the late 19th and early 20th centuries[3] .

---

[3] Lest there be any doubt: in previous research we have referred to the greatness of Niklas Luhman's thinking. This is by no means abandoned. But it is not because we have chosen one author for our research that the others have not done great work. What's more, although Luhmann is an author whose thinking invades many areas, he is not a philosopher (at least not from a conservative perspective). He engages in various debates with philosophy, and his theoretical basis is strongly grounded in these debates, which demonstrates his great knowledge in this area, including his writings on man, the human being, the person. As for Martin Heidegger, there is no doubt that he is one of the most important philosophers. Therefore, as we have chosen to complement the blind spots in our observation of judicial decision-making, there is nothing better than to extend the analysis from a Heideggerian point of view, as some of his most important concerns are the same as Luhmann's. This relationship

After a crisis in global theories, especially those linked to absolute thought (empiricists and rationalists), a breakdown of philosophical thought began in Europe[4]. Between 1910 and 1920, neo-philosophies began to emerge (neo-Kantism, neo-Marxism, among others), which led to the reinvigoration of theories of knowledge, which had a fundamental problem: how can knowledge be justified?

In order to answer this fundamental question in the philosophical world, which has repercussions in all other areas, two opposing currents gained strength in the period. In a nutshell, it can be said that one of them sought to answer the problem through logic and language (the Vienna School), of which Ludwig Wittgenstein is the greatest exponent[5]. The other school rejected scientific and purely logical explanations, believing that the answer to the great question of the period lay, for example, in the phenomenology of Edmund Husserl.[6].

It was in the midst of these philosophical currents, which still maintained the separation between subject and object, that Martin Heidegger developed a new way of understanding man and the world, which he called Existential Analytics. He was introduced to this discussion when he became Husserl's

---

between the two theories is the same. This relationship between the theories is part of the author's doctoral thesis, which will soon be published.

[4] STRECK, Lenio Luiz. Heidegger, Martin, 1889-1976. IN: BARRETTO, Vicente de Paulo (Org.), *Dicionario* de *Filosofia do Direito*. Sao Leopoldo: Editora Unisinos; Rio de Janeiro/RJ: Livraria Editora Renovar, 2009. p. 426-27.

[5] It is important to note here that the author is only linked to this philosophical current in its first phase, in which the most important book is Treatise on Philosophical Logic. However, it should not be forgotten that Wittgenstein has a second phase, in which he makes severe changes to his previous positions, with the book Investigagoes Filosoficas (Philosophical Investigations). WITTGENSTEIN. Ludwing. *Logico-Philosophical Treatise; Philosophical Investigations*. Translated by M. S. Lourengo. 3.ed. Lisbon: Calouste Gulbenkian Foundation, 2002.

[6] It should be noted that phenomenology was born with Husserl, but it was still linked to

consciousness.

HUSSERL, Edmund. *Logical Investigations: Sixth Investigation: Elements of a Phenomenological Elucidation of Knowledge.* Translated by Ziljko Loparic and Andrea Maria Altino de Campos Loparic. Sao Paulo: Nova Cultural, 1998 (The Thinkers).

assistant.[7] Husserl's assistant, and was thus able to follow the development of his master's theory, as well as the discussions that took place between the scholars. By following the development of Hussellian phenomenology, Heidegger was able to see that, although it sought to overcome some issues, it was still stuck in the subject-object schema, which prevented a more in-depth analysis of the problem in question.

In this vein, Heidegger follows Husserl's proposals but develops a theory of his own, in which philosophy ceases to concern itself only with beings and begins to concern itself with Being. From the moment this step is taken, Heidegger also separates Being from Being. This will imply, among other things, the overcoming of the subject-object schema.

In this way, a new phase of philosophy would be inaugurated, which has not yet been surpassed by Philosophy[8]. To develop his proposal, the German philosopher uses a unique way of writing: questioning, interrogative, with language that is often athermological and even poetic.[9]. His questions are not at all innovative, but the way they are posed and how they are answered are

---

[7] Born on September 26, 1889, Heidegger studied philosophy and theology (with theology being much more a result of his economic circumstances which, from the beginning of his studies, forced him to opt for training in religious colleges, the only possibility of meeting the costs, since the Church paid for the training of those who were preparing for a career in the priesthood, a situation that ended only in 1919). After serving as Husserl's assistant, he succeeded the master in his philosophy chair in Freiburg. A few years later, in 1933, he became Rector of that institution. He wrote several works, but his most important is undoubtedly Being and Time. For a complete bibliography, see SAFRANSKI, RODIGER. *Heidegger: a German master between good and evil*. Translated by Lya Lett Luft. Sao Paulo: Geragao Editorial, 2005. Further information in REALE, Giovani; ANTISERI, Dario. *History of Philosophy: From Romanticism to the present day*. Vol. 3. Sao Paulo: Paulus, 1991.p, 581-82.

[8] It should be noted that for authors from other areas, this overcoming can and has occurred in other ways. An example of this is Luhmann's work on the place of individuals in systems theory. For this, see the text WEBBER, Suelen. *Observagoes sobre a forma pessoa e seus reflexos para o Sistema do Direito e da Politica*, to be published in the next volume of Anpof.

[9] An example of this is when he talks about "unveiling", "clearing of being", "desert of being", "abyss of being", "silent call", or makes analogies, as can be seen in this passage: "In what soil do the roots of the tree of philosophy find their support? From what ground do the roots and, through them, the whole tree receive their sap and nourishing forces? What is the element that runs hidden in the soil, the roots that support and nourish the tree? On what does metaphysics rest and move? What is metaphysics seen from its foundation? What, in the final analysis, is metaphysics?" HEIDEGGER, Martin. *Philosophical lectures and writings*. Translated by Vergilio Ferreira. São Paulo: Victor Civita, 1973. (Os Pensadores, XLV). p. 253. Published with Existentialism and Humanism; Imagination; Question of Method, all by Jean-Paul Sartre.

(including answers that become new questions).[10]. The words commonly used in the world of philosophical writing can no longer express what needs to be said through the textual event[11]The words used in philosophical writing can no longer express what needs to be said through the text event, but their spelling needs to be modified to give them new unique meanings - with the addition of hyphens, for example - and when this is no longer enough, new words will be created by it (like Dasein).

Having said that, perhaps this is the moment to ask why the question of Being (and thus the separation between Being and being) is so important and what its implication is in the discussion posed at the beginning: the (in)authenticity and (ir)responsibility of judges when deciding. The answer is already outlined in the first paragraph of Being and Time[12]Heidegger's main work.

It is precisely in the first few lines of this book that the philosopher sets out why the question of Being must be re-examined, and why it must now be re-examined in a different way than the pre-socratics did. Here he states that they posed the question in the wrong way, because "all metaphysics has thought about being while claiming to be Being. What metaphysics called Being was actually being".[13]. Therefore, from Heidegger's perspective, we know that not even *being* was thought of in this logic, because we only have

---

[10]   Here we have a direct similarity with the author Niklas Luhmann.

[11]   According to Streck: "Text and event!; texts do not produce 'virtual realities'; texts are not mere linguistic utterances; texts are not words in the wind, metaphysical concepts that do not concern something (something like something). This is the specificity of law: texts are important; texts matter to us". STRECK, Lenio Luiz. *Truth and Consensus: Constitution, Hermeneutics and Discursive Theories*. 4.ed. São Paulo: Saraiva, 2011. p. 219. Gadamer, in the same vein, states that: "Whoever 'understands' a text (or even a law) has not only projected himself into a meaning by understanding - in the effort to understand - but the understanding achieved represents the state of a new spiritual freedom. It implies the possibility of interpreting, detecting relationships, drawing conclusions in all directions, etc., which is what constitutes understanding the subject within the field of understanding texts". GADAMER, Hans-Georg. Truth and Method I: *Fundamental Traces of a Philosophical Hermeneutics*. Translated by Flavio Paulo Meurer and Enio Paulo Giachini. 11.ed. Braganga Paulista: Editora Universitaria Sao Franciso; Petropolis: Editora Vozes, 2011. p. 348-49.

[12]   HEIDEGGER, Martin. *Sein undZeit*. Tubingen: Max Niemeyer Verlag, 2006.

[13]   STRECK. Lenio Luiz. *Truth and Consensus: Constitution, Hermeneutics and Discursive Theories*. 4.ed. Sao Paulo: Saraiva, 2011.p. 215.

access to being while it is *being*, and in order for it to be, we need to know Being.

> What is at issue in the question we need to elaborate is that being, that which determines the entity as entity, that with a view to which the entity, in whatever form it is considered, is always already understood. The being of the being is not, the same being[14]

In this passage, you can get an idea of how this question is relayed, so that with Herve Pasqua you can formulate that: "Being is not being and yet being is! What is the nature of this difference?"[15] Faced with Pasqua's question, a bigger question arises, which is at the heart of the entire incursion proposed here: what does it mean to say that a thing *IS*? How can we say what law *is*, what a human being *is*, what chalk *is*[16] ? This is the question that has been attempted to be answered throughout *Being and Time.* This is why this point is fundamental to solving the problem posed and analyzing the many others arising from it and connected to it: we need to know what things are, so that we can then analyze them, and thus get rid of false ideas, such as obviousness and prejudices.

At this point, Heidegger himself will say that, in order to unveil Being, three prejudices need to be broken down. Then we can go on to answer other questions, even the most banal ones. The first prejudice to be broken would be the assertion that *Being is the most universal concept and therefore the clearest'* [7]. Now, being the most universal concept does not lead to the conclusion that it is the clearest, much less that it is self-evident. It was with this in mind that until now we had never thought of Being and being as a

---

[14] HEIDEGGER, Martin. Sein und Zeit. 19. ed. Tubingen: Max Niemeyer Verlag, 2006. p. 6.

[15] PASQUA, Herve. *Introduction to Martin Heidegger's Being and Time.* Translated by Joana Chaves. Lisbon: Instituto Piaget, 1995. p. 9.

[16] The chalk object will become our exemplifying entity, in order to be faithful to the examples worked on by Heidegger in his book Introduction to Philosophy.

distinct unity.

As a result of this first prejudice, the statement that would become the second prejudice emerged: "the concept of being is indefinable".[17][18]and therefore, if Being were universal, this would make it indefinable. The answer given to these critics is that, in fact, Being cannot be conceived as an entity, nor can it be determined by adding an entity to it. Being is something distinct from being, and therefore the way of determining beings, justified within the limits of traditional logic, cannot be applied to Being.

And as a third obstacle, we have to face the proposition that "Being is a self-evident concept"[19]Therefore, when something is conceptualized or qualified, there is already an implicit understanding of Being. The answer to this is that "this common understanding only demonstrates incomprehension"[20]In fact, what happens is that everyone has a pre-understanding of Being, but no one questions its meaning. Appearing evident makes it an enigma, and this further legitimizes the question that drives the investigation with the distinction between Being and being.

However, more important than overcoming the prejudices established since antiquity about Being, perhaps the most innovative aspect of Heidegger's question about Being lies in the formal structure of the correct question about Being. And that the way in which a question is posed immediately indicates the path to the solution.

In this way, it should be considered that "every question is a search. Every search removes its previous direction from what is sought. To question

---

[17] HEIDEGGER, Martin. *Sein und Zeit.* 19. ed. Tubingen: Max Niemeyer Verlag, 2006. p. 3. In the first paragraph of Being and Time, in order to justify the importance and necessity of re-examining the question of Being, Heidegger analyzes the three prejudices that need to be overcome.

[18] HEIDEGGER, Martin. *Sein undZeit.* 19. ed. Tubingen: Max Niemeyer Verlag, 2006. p. 4.

[19] HEIDEGGER, Martin. *Sein undZeit.* 19. ed. Tubingen: Max Niemeyer Verlag, 2006. p. 4.

[20] *HEIDEGGER,* Martin. Sein und Zeit. 19. ed. Tubingen: Max Niemeyer Verlag, 2006. p. 4.

is to seek the being in what it is as it is". It so happens that when a question is asked, a pre-understanding of what is being questioned is already assumed on the part of the questioner, and the object sought by the question must be accessible in some way. In other words, when you question the (in)authenticity of the judge when he decides based solely on other decisions, without adequate reasoning, you already have a prior understanding of what you're trying to explore, because if you're willing to do this, it's because what you're looking for isn't totally unknown. But this will not lead to any paradox or self-evident investigation, precisely because the distinction between Being and being allows the figure of Dasein to emerge, which will prevent this paradox, allowing being to ask about Being.

This is in line with what was said in the first lines of this paper: you don't have direct access to Being, but only through the being, since when the being shows itself, the Being shows itself. What's more, in order to elucidate the meaning, you can't have just Being and being in this relationship without an interlocutor who is Dasein, because if you do that and ask, for example, what the judge's responsibility *is*, you would be transforming Being into a being, and that would give us a false answer.

From the moment we start talking about Dasein, it is necessary to study this Dasein. It occupies a privileged place in this relationship between Being and being, being the only one capable of questioning the meaning of Being, without creating paradoxes or a failure to unveil meaning. Thus, studying it is fundamental in order to understand its relationship with other beings, which is what will make this philosophy of Being and Time different: a philosophy designed for the Being of Dasein, and no longer for the subject (and therefore overcoming the subject-object relationship).

In order to understand Dasein, we must first understand the task of ontology[21]. To explain this relationship of distinction between Being and being

---

[21]   HEIDEGGER, Martin. *Sein undZeit.* 19. ed. Tubingen: Max Niemeyer Verlag, 2006. p. 27.

in order to explain Being. Scientific methods in general fail to do this, and start describing phenomena rather than explaining why something *IS* or *ISN'T* in a certain way. In other words, all scientific methods end up being concerned with what is, and are therefore ontic[22]. However, in order to reach Being (and thus understand the role of Dasein), a method (or discipline, as Gadamer would say) will be needed that is suited to what we are trying to achieve. For this reason, it won't be a scientific method, but the phenomenological method[23]. "Ontology is only possible as phenomenology (...). Phenomenology is letting and making see from itself what is shown, as it is shown from itself".[24].

With this, Heidegger goes further, and, since Dasein is the dimension from which beings are given as such, in which the meaning of Being manifests itself, the ontology that seeks to elucidate the structure of Dasein must be understood as a fundamental ontology. In order to understand this fundamental ontology, Heidegger makes an interesting confrontation between his own theory and the theories of Aristotle and Kant. This can be seen in one

---

[22] It was along these lines that Gadamer wrote his most famous work Truth and Method, precisely to combat the idea that truth was in the method or that it depended on it. Without access to Being, it would not be possible to obtain the truth, and therefore the Truth would not be in the Method. "What the 'instrumental' 'method' cannot achieve must and can indeed be achieved by a discipline of asking and investigating that guarantees truth." GADAMER, Hans-Georg. Truth and Method I: *Fundamental outlines of a philosophical hermeneutics*. Translated by Flavio Paulo Meurer and Enio Paulo Giachini. 11.ed. Braganpa Paulista: Editora Universitaria Sao Franciso; Petropolis: Editora Vozes, 2011, p. 631.

[23] To clarify the issue: in the phenomenological method, you start from the things themselves and the way in which they appear in order to know them. For rationalists, for example, you have all the concepts and things remind you of these concepts. For empiricists, on the other hand, you are born as a blank page, and as you go through life, you fill in these pages through experience. HESSE, Johannes. *The Theory of Knowledge*. Sao Paulo: Martins Fontes, 2000. Here, it is worth noting another difference between Husserl's phenomenology and Heidegger's. For Husserl, the process of perceiving phenomena takes place from the transcendental self. For Heidegger, however, phenomenology is hermeneutic because it is linked to the understanding of phenomena and of Dasein, in an interrelationship between Dasein and the understanding of Being. STEIN, Ernildo. *Introduction to the thought of Martin Heidegger*. Porto Alegre: EDIPUCRS, 2002. p. 53-4.

[24] HEIDEGGER, Martin. *Sein undZeit*. 19. ed. Tubingen: Max Niemeyer Verlag, 2006. p. 34-5.

of his lectures [25].

The question is, then, what is the basis for the possibility of man being questioned by being as being, that is, why can being itself become open to man in the sense of presence? But the manifestation [Offenbarkeit] of being for man absolutely does not mean that being as such, or even its manifestation, is understood thematically by man and by the thinking of philosophy.

The question then arises: How must man's being be placed so that the determination of man corresponds to the fundamental phenomenon of the manifestation of being? Where does the understanding come from that man himself is in this clearing of being, in other words, that the being of ai [Da] is ekstalic, that man exists as Da-sein?

The interpretation of the main structures that make up the being of the being thus placed, that is, its existence, is the existential analysis of Dasein. The term *existential* is used interchangeably with categorical. Category in modern usage means a class or group to which certain things belong. For example: he belongs to this or that category. Category comes from the Greek verb ayopeueiv, which means to speak publicly in the marketplace (...), especially matters of justice. The preposition κατα means from above towards something, the same thing as our "about"; to say *something* about something, in the special case of the public trial in the indictment, to say something directly to the accused. So KaTqyopia actually means declaration. In Aristotle KaTqyopia is given the meaning of those determinations that belong to the declaration as such. Something about which I state something, the subject of the sentence, belongs to the statement. What *is* stated about (...) *is* the predicate. In the statement I say, for example, something has such and such properties; property [Beschaffenheit] is the category of quality. Something has such a height or width. How much, as such, is called the category of quantity. The number of categories in Aristotle varies. In any case, these categories are not simple determinations of the ability to understand, as in Kant, but characters of the being of the entity as such. The same thing applies, of course, to Kant too, except that for him the presence of what is present took on the meaning of the objectivity of the object.

In *Being and Time, I* tried to show the specific characters of being of Dasein as Dasein in comparison with the characters of being of that which does not have the character of Dasein, for example, nature, and therefore

I called them *existential. **Dasein's analysis of Dasein is, as an existential, formally speaking, a kind of ontology. Since it is that ontology which prepares the fundamental question of being as being, it is a fundamental ontology. This makes it clear, again, that understanding Being and Time as an anthropology is a misinterpretation.*** (no emphasis in the original).

---

[25] We say lectures because the book Seminars at Zollikon is a compilation of transcripts of lectures given by Heidegger in the years between 1947 and 1949 at Zollikon, as well as letters exchanged between Heidegger and Medard Boss. HEIDEGGER, Martin. *Zollikon Seminars: protocols, dialogues, letters.* Translated by Gabriella Arnhold and Maria de Fatima de Almeida Prado. 2.ed. Braganpa Paulista: Editora Universitaria Sao Francisco; Petropolis: Editora Vozes, 2009.

The long quote is justified. From it, it can be said that the study of the constitutive structures of this being that is Dasein (or, more precisely, of the Being of this being) is what Heidegger called fundamental ontology. Existential analysis, on the other hand, will be an analysis of the structure of Dasein and the characteristics of this entity (Dasein) will be called existential, while the characteristics of other entities will be categories or categorical. Let's start with Dasein.

Dasein, as mentioned earlier, is a word created by Heidegger to provide an explanation that did not fit into any word in the German language until then. This sometimes leads to communication problems, as the translation of the term becomes complicated and can sometimes affect and compromise its meaning. In simple terms, it can be said that *Da* is translated as *af,* indicating an openness in which man understands himself and the world, projecting himself as a possibility onto himself[26][27]while *Sein* means *Being.* In other words, it's about openness, the breadth of Being.

Dasein means being together with things, with the world, not physically, but ontologically. In other words, Dasein is not just an entity in the midst of other entities. On the contrary, Heidegger sees Dasein as the only entity capable of asking questions about Being, because it is in a privileged position in relation to other entities. Although it participates in the world as an entity - and therefore ontically - Dasein also has an ontological dimension.

> All the objectifying encapsulated representations of a psyche, a subject, a person, an I, a consciousness, used up to now in psychology and psychopathology, must disappear in the analytical vision of the Da-sein in favor of a completely different understanding. The fundamental constitution of human existence to be considered from now on will be called *Da-sein* or *being-in-the-world.* However, the *Da of* this *Dasein* does not mean, as is often the case, a place in the space close to the observer. What existing as *Da-sein* means is keeping open an ambit of being able to grasp the meanings of what appears or is spoken of from its clearing. The human Da-sein as an ambit of power-understanding *is*

---

[26] HEIDEGGER, Martin. *Zollikon Seminars: Protocols, Dialogues, Letters.* Translated by Gabriella Arnhold and Maria de Fatima de Almeida Prado. 2.ed. Braganpa Paulista: Editora Universitaria Sao Francisco; Petropolis: Editora Vozes, 2009. p. 160-61.
[27] TUGENDHAT, Ernest. *Self-consciousness and Self-determination: a linguistic-analytical interpretation.* Madrid: FCE, 1993.

never simply a present object. On the contrary, it is in no way and under no circumstances something that can be objectified [28].

Dasein is a being. Although Dasein is one of Heidegger's most mentioned terms, it is not a Being, but an entity, the entity of Man. For Heidegger, a distinction must also be made between Being and being in man, and this will mean that Dasein is the being, while Care is the Being of this Man.

Essentially, Dasein is the possibility of being. Possibility of Being is the possibility of languishing in projects, which are the ability to languish in the future while remaining in the present. Thus, Dasein will come into being in the realization of this project, in the possibility of the realization of this langement in the future, of this projection, because Dasein can exist in innumerable ways. And the Being of Dasein is not something given in advance, but is only revealed to the extent that Dasein assumes what Heidegger called modes of being. Therefore, it is in assuming modes of being that Dasein *is.* So, it is up to Dasein to decide how to be.

In this sense, it seems pertinent to mention the considerations of David Webb for this work:

> (...) for Heidegger, it is only when Dasein projects itself upon the horizon of its own mortality and the totality of Dasein's potentiality-for-Being is disclosed as a whole (e.g. in anxiety), that Dasein can come back to itself in such a way as to disclose the possibilities within the totality of its existence precisely as possibilities that belong essentially to its own existence [29].

Temporal finitude, revealed in being-for-death[30]presents itself to Dasein

---

[28] HEIDEGGER, Martin. *Zollikon Seminars: protocols, dialogues, letters.* Translated by Gabriella Arnhold and Maria de Fatima de Almeida Prado. 2.ed. Braganga Paulista: Editora Universitaria Sao Francisco; Petropolis: Editora Vozes, 2009. p. 33.

[29] WEBB, David. *Heidegger, Ethics and the Practice of Ontology.* London/New York: Continuum Studies in Continental Philosophy, 2009. p. 116. Free translation: "(...) for Heidegger, it is only when Dasein projects itself onto the horizon of its own mortality and the totality of Dasein's potentiality-for-being is unveiled as a whole (e.g. in anguish), that Dasein can return to itself in such a way as to unveil the possibilities in the totality of its existence precisely as possibilities that essentially belong to its own existence."

[30] For a more detailed look at being-for-death, see WEBBER, Marcos Andre. *Ethics and Existence:*

as the possibility of the impossibility of Being. Therefore, in projecting itself, Dasein always has the possibility of no longer being. And understanding the anticipation of death allows Dasein to understand its Being as a whole, calling Dasein to assume itself and its own existence. It is not, however, an ontic death, but an ontological one; man not only dies, but ceases to be.

It is also important to note that, while Dasein can assume infinite modes of being - since there are infinite ways of being - it is essential to realize that it cannot not be (as Webb showed us). It has to be at all times. By not deciding on his mode of being, he can fall into the inauthentic mode of being, which, although it is also a mode of being, and also constitutes an existential (and then Dasein will still be being), it will have other peculiarities, which will be better explored in chapter two of this book.

To resume. The whole possibility of Dasein's being takes place in the world. In other words, there is no Dasein that is not, is not in the world. Being-in-the-world is in the very constitution of Dasein[31]. In the same way, being-with-others, being-in, being-for-death, being-culpable, are all existentials that highlight Dasein's characteristic of Being.

This also highlights Heidegger's proposal to overcome the subject versus object schema, so much so that, at a certain point in his work, he poses the following question: "Haven't we simply established another word for the same being, being-there instead of subject?"[32]And after some analysis, he concludes that it is patently not. After all, we're not nominalists! Dasein is not simply an entity that is thrown into the world alongside other entities and relates to them. In the very constitution of Dasein, there is already a co-

---

a *Heudeggerian contribution*. Caxias do Sul: EDUCS, 2016.

[31] The world is not something that joins Dasein from the outside like a being to another being. The world is part of Dasein's being, and has an essential relationship with it. In Heidegger's words: "Being-in is therefore the formal existential expression of the being of Dasein, which has the essential constitution of being-in-the-world." HEIDEGGER, Martin. *Sein und Zeit*. 19. ed. Tubingen: Max Niemeyer Verlag, 2006. p. 54.

[32] HEIDEGGER, Martin. *Introduction to Philosophy*. Translated by Marco Antonio Casanova. Sao Paulo: Martins Fontes, 2009. p. 76.

pertaining between Dasein and the world.

According to Heidegger, human nature is stripped of any stable attribute. Dasein is not a thing, nor a substance, nor an object, nor a subject. It has no essence before its existence. That is, Dasein exists first, and from its existence it forges its essence. Attention: the essence we are talking about here is not a metaphysical essence, like the essence in Sartre, for example[33]but an essence in the ontological sense[34]. That is to say: it is by existing, within its possibilities of being-in-the-world, that Dasein constitutes its Being. Furthermore, the Being of Dasein is always the Being of that Dasein, which is different from the Being of other Daseins, because every Dasein is a Dasein. Thus, the Being of Dasein is always singular and distinct from others.

So, in fact, Dasein is free to project itself, within the possibilities that surround facticity, because it is the realization of countless project possibilities, but this has no relation to will, to wanting, to subjectivity and consciousness.

To delve deeper into these issues and get to our original question about the (in)authenticity and responsibility of the judges, it is the Being of Dasein that deserves to be highlighted: Care (*Sorge*). To make the approach more didactic, we could venture to say that Care is the Being of man, while Dasein would be his being. However, as man has no essence prior to his existence, and his nature has no stable attribute (which would be the same as speaking of a prior essence), we prefer to say that Care is the Being of Dasein.

Rafael Tomaz de Oliveira offers us a very interesting approach to Care and the threefold structure that makes it up ontologically. In the author's words:

---

[33] With Sartre, there is only the inversion of the relationship between essence and existence, but he is still stuck with the subject-object opposition that Heidegger wants to overcome. SARTRE, Jean-Paul. *Being and Nothingness: An Essay in Phenomenological Ontology.* Translated by Paulo Perdigao. 5. ed. Petropolis: Vozes, 1997.

[34] PASQUA, Herve. *Introduction to Martin Heidegger's Being and Time.* Translated by Joana Chaves. Lisbon: Instituto Piaget, 1995. p. 38-9.

1) ja-ser-em - which indicates facticity, being thrown into a world (facticity);
2) being-forward-of-itself - which implies existence, the possibilities that Dasein has to decide on;
3) being-together-with-things - which indicates decay.
The triple structure of care will then unfold in the triple dimension of temporality: past (facticity); future (existence); and present (decay).[35].

In this sense, facticity is finding oneself in a set of possibilities of being already given in existence. They are the situations of being already given in existence. It is the particular and specific situation of each Dasein at a given moment. When we talk about the possibilities that Dasein has to decide, it is necessary to refer again to the notion that Dasein always has to be and, therefore, this will be its existentiality within its possibilities of Being. Finally, decay (or dependence) is being together with the totality of beings (physically)[36].

On the other hand, we could say that facticity is past - and past, present and future occur in the same non-linear instant - because when we are in a given situation, what led to that situation are exactly the facts that have already happened. The future will be included in the project precisely because it is the capacity to be (and existence produces essence). Finally, the present is the decay because it is being with beings physically, and *being* can only be in the present. There is no way to be in the future or the past, but only in the present. This is the triple temporal dimension.

Although there are several existentials that underpin Dasein, they are not dispersed parts of one being. On the contrary, existentials must be understood as a unity, and what allows them to be understood as an intrinsic unity of the multiplicity of existentials is Care, starting from Anguish.

This anguish, however, should not be understood in the psychological

---

[35] OLIVEIRA, RAFAEL Tomaz de. *Decisao Judicial e o conceito* de *principio: a hermeneutica e a (in) determinapao do Direito.* Porto Alegre: Livraria do Advogado, 2008. p. 158.

[36] See HAAR, Michel. *Heidegger and the essence of man.* Translated by Ana Cristina Alves. Lisbon: Instituto Piaget. 1997. p. 21.

sense, nor does it relate to the fear that Dasein feels when it is threatened by an entity, but it is an existential anguish. But what does "existential anguish" mean? That's what we'll see in the next chapter.

CHAPTER II

How inauthenticity can give rise to the camouflage of metaphysics in the decision-making process: the necessary rescue by anguish

In the first chapter of this book, introductory notes were made on the work of Martin Heidegger, from which we sought to understand some unique situations of judgments in the Brazilian judiciary, including: what is the responsibility (not legal, but hermeneutic) of the judge when deciding? That chapter ended by analyzing Care *(Sorge)* and its relationship with anguish. It therefore seems prudent to return to this point, which is fundamental to the analysis of authenticity and inauthenticity, central elements in the proposed communication.

In Heidegger, anguish is the existential that shows Dasein its particular situation - its particular way of being - and therefore opens up the possibility of seeing its situation in a unique way. It opens up the possibility for Dasein to realize that it is, and that it moves in such a way as to want to escape from the Impersonal or from what is also known as *the people,* or even the *das Man.*

It is therefore the "inauthenticity" of *Dasein.* Inauthentic *Dasein* does not live as itself, but as "they live". But it lives. It is lived. In inauthentic existence, we are constantly afraid of other people's opinions, of what "they" will decide for us, of not living up to the standards of material or psychological success, even though we have done nothing to establish or even verify these standards. This fear is what is known as *furcht.*

Angst, however, differently and radically, is one of the primary instruments through which the character and the ontic context of everyday existence inevitably become aware of the pressures of the ontological. *Angst* is thus a mark of authenticity, of repudiation of otherness. The "se" *(man)* tends to understand the world according to the opinions of others, according to the public mentality. Even when, concretely, within the scheme of the "if", we distance ourselves from the "great mass" because "they" distance themselves from it; we find scandalous what "they" find scandalous [37].

This impersonality is nothing more than inauthenticity, that way of being in which people say "I do it this way because everyone else does it this way." I am like this because everyone else is like this". Or, as we propose to analyze, "I decide like this because the Court has already decided like this"! "Even against my personal position[38] I vote with the rapporteur for the sake of speed and procedural economy".

For Hommerding, when Dasein assumes this mode of being (which is inauthentic, as you can see), it is denying its being. It is not being itself. Anguish calls Dasein to assume its own being and to be itself. Dasein realizes its way of being and its possibilities of being and is then able to project itself as itself.

> Anguish is the condition of possibility for an authentic life. Since its being-in-the-world belongs ontologically to *Dasein,* its being towards the world must essentially be occupation *(sorge)* and preoccupation *(besorgen).* Being-there only becomes visible as *sorge* [39].

Here there is a conjunction with Care, because Care can be understood as an anticipation of oneself, in which Dasein projects itself, launches itself into the future as a possibility of being and then returns to be able to realize the project. It should be noted that Care and project are not to be confused. Care is prior to the project. Care is the condition of possibility for the project.

As mentioned earlier, Dasein assumes modes of being. At this point,

---

[37] HOMMERDING, Adalberto Narciso. Paragraph 3 of Article 515 of the Civil Procedure Code: an analysis in the light of the hermeneutic philosophy (or philosophical hermeneutics) of Heidegger and Gadamer. IN: *Revista da AJURIS/Associagao dos Juizes do Rio Grande do Sul* - v. 30, n. 91. Porto Alegre: AJURIS, Sep. 2003. p. 21.

[38] Of course, "personal position" is not understood here as a decision I want to make, but in the sense that often, even if the judge has a legal understanding, given by the context, that differs from that of the other members of the Chamber, he prefers to omit it so as not to break the hegemony of the Panel or even so as not to have to present his reasons in a convincing process (and therefore responsibility) to the other colleagues, often just to speed up the process.

[39] HOMMERDING, Adalberto Narciso. Paragraph 3 of Article 515 of the Civil Procedure Code: an analysis in the light of the hermeneutic philosophy (or philosophical hermeneutics) of Heidegger and Gadamer. IN: *Revista da AJURIS/Associagao dos Juizes do Rio Grande do Sul* - v. 30, n. 91. Porto Alegre: AJURIS, Sep. 2003. p. 22.

what is most relevant to our study is the fact that these modes of being can be authentic or inauthentic.

When, in everyday life, Dasein "goes on living", simply existing, without realizing its particular and unique situation in the world, Dasein takes on ways of being that are common to all Daseins, it is being inauthentic. In this situation, Dasein ceases to be itself and falls into what Heidegger calls *das Man,* which is the impersonal, the "we", "us". This is an existence outside oneself, without taking responsibility for one's own being.

> Here we begin to distinguish authentic existence from inauthentic existence. The inauthentic being-there is incapable of truly opening up to things. It doesn't possess that purity and conformity with fact which are proper to discourse and understanding. Authenticity *(Eigenlichkeit)* is taken by Heidegger in its literal etymological sense, in connection with the adjective *"eigen".* Authentic is the being-there that appropriates itself, in other words, that projects itself onto the basis of its most own possibility. We can therefore determine the average everydayness of Dasein as a being-in-the-world open to de-cadence which, in a languorous way, projects itself and which, in its being in the world and in its being-with-others, its most proper power-to-be is at stake[40] .

And this is exactly the point to be explored.

Heidegger says that everyone tends to fall into this inauthentic mode of being[41] , because the impersonal is also an existential. It is said that existence "is a <<passage>>, a passage into the world, in which the being of Dasein resides".[42]. Therefore, inauthenticity, although it is a way of being, is only a passage, a moment, but not a continuity, in which Dasein develops its own possibilities for existing authentically. You have to go through it, but you don't have to remain in authenticity continuously, because the German philosopher warns that the tranquillity of unconcern that takes Dasein in its inauthentic way

---

[40] HOMMERDING, Adalberto Narciso. Paragraph 3 of Article 515 of the Civil Procedure Code: an analysis in the light of the hermeneutic philosophy (or philosophical hermeneutics) of Heidegger and Gadamer. IN: *Revista da AJURIS/Associaqao dos Juizes do Rio Grande do Sul* - v. 30, n. 91. Porto Alegre: AJURIS, Sep. 2003. p. 21.

[41] In particular, in paragraphs 27 and 38 of Being and Time.

[42] PASQUA, Herve. *Introduction to Martin Heidegger's Being and Time.* Translated by Joana Chaves. Lisbon: Instituto Piaget, 1995. p. 92.

of being is so fleeting that even in inauthenticity, Dasein begins to be disturbed, to worry, and will need to return to being authentic. Dasein begins to exist in the impersonal, and it is from this that the change to authenticity must emerge, from the moment Dasein realizes this inauthenticity and takes on Being itself. "The fall is not at stake, but the power to be-in-the-world, albeit in the mode of impropriety"[43].

Thus, it can be said that inauthenticity is an escape, a flight by Dasein from its fears and responsibilities.

> *Dasein* runs away, gets distracted, and gets caught up in an agitated action. At the outset, it finds itself trapped in this game. But he doesn't yet know that this escape, this distraction, is not an escape from his condition, but his own condition. He will begin to live authentically when he realizes that being is ek-sistir, and that he is free-falling into the nothingness of death. This is the very thing (eigen) of authentic existence (eigentlich).[44].

Although everyone has a tendency to fall into this inauthentic way of being, we have to see that this can happen without any major problems while we are in banal situations in our lives, when we are making choices (choosing a drink - I'd like a juice, but everyone is drinking soda, what to wear - I don't like a certain style, but it's what's in fashion). However, while we are in the position of judge, of someone who decides, this impersonality must be removed in order to make this decision[45]. From this perspective, we must

---

[43] HEIDEGGER, Martin. *Sein undZeit.* 19. ed. Tubingen: Max Niemeyer Verlag, 2006. p. 179.

[44] PASQUA, Herve. *Introduction to Martin Heidegger's Being and Time.* Translated by Joana Chaves. Lisbon: Instituto Piaget, 1995. p. 93.

[45] Heidegger has already told us that it is only in everyday life that one can be inauthentic."Above it has been shown that the immediate surrounding world is always already within reach, as the object of common occupation, the public 'surrounding world'. In the use of public transportation, in the use of information services (newspapers), everyone is the same as everyone else. This way of living together completely dissuades one's own Dasein in the way of being 'of others', and this to such an extent that the others disappear even more as they are

conclude that in order to decide, we need to unveil meaning, and the unveiling of meaning and the ability to take responsibility will only happen in the authentic way of being. Therefore, as a judge, in the moment of decision, inauthenticity must be ruled out. "That's why, when the judge decides using, for example, 'calm and peaceful jurisprudence', he is not the one who is deciding, that is, he is not the one who has the responsibility"[46]. Note the subtlety of the issue for us. The problem does not lie in the fact that you use "settled case law", but rather that you do not clearly state in your decision why in that specific case you should use "settled case law" as an argument for your decision. What does this mean? That the (hermeneutic and democratic) problem is to accommodate oneself and only refer to "settled case law", without at least justifying why! And many decisions are handed down in this way.

Attention is drawn to the fact that, although Heidegger admits that everyone tends to fall into this impersonal mode, he is not saying that it is advisable to always live in this impersonal mode. Attention: the impersonal is a condition of possibility for authenticity, because it calls, it makes it possible to take over the reins once again and take responsibility, but it is not a permanent mode of being. The inauthentic is the condition for the authentic in this game of unveilings, but it is not the appropriate way of being, because it represents an equivocal understanding of Being. This is because, "inauthenticity designates nothing so much as a not-being-in-the-world that

---

distinguished and made explicit. Without drawing attention to itself and without being noticed, it establishes a veritable dictatorship. We enjoy and have fun the way *he* does; we read, watch and judge literature and art the way *he* does; but we also stay away from the 'moton' the way he should; we find 'annoying' what he should find annoying. The us, which is not a particular person and which is everyone (but not as the sum of all), prescribes the way of being in everyday life".
HEIDEGGER, Martin. *Sein und Zeit.* 19. ed. Tubingen: Max Niemeyer Verlag, 2006. p. 127.

[46] HOMMERDING, Adalberto Narciso. Paragraph 3 of Article 515 of the Civil Procedure Code: an analysis in the light of the hermeneutic philosophy (or philosophical hermeneutics) of Heidegger and Gadamer. IN: *Revista da AJURIS/Associaqao dos Julzes do Rio Grande do* Sul - v. 30, n. 91. Porto Alegre: AJURIS, Sep. 2003. p. 20.

constitutes precisely a privileged being-in-the-world that is completely taken over by the world".[47].

Therefore, when Dasein hears the call of its conscience, when it realizes that it is assuming inauthentic ways of being, it takes its Being for itself and opens up the possibility of linking itself to the future (as a project) in an authentic way - it launches itself from its singular situation - and decides for itself what it wants to Be. Then Dasein is being itself, and can be said to be authentic.

This consciousness, however, is not the consciousness of a subject and certainly not the isolated and solipsistic consciousness of a judge.[48]of a judge. It simply calls Dasein[49]so that Dasein can "become aware" of the modes of being it is assuming, and that it must decide for itself how to be. By remaining in the "we", Dasein fails to take responsibility for its own Being. Listening to the call of consciousness, Dasein is called upon to assume itself and thus be able to define its Being authentically.

> This call would break the listening of the "us" in which Dasein does not listen to itself and if it manages to awaken, by virtue of its own call, a listening of entirely different characteristics from the listening lost in the "us". If the latter is confused by the 'turmoil' and misunderstanding of the ever 'new' daily chatter, the call must call out silently and unequivocally,

---

[47] PASQUA, Herve. *An introduction to Martin Heidegger's Being and Time.* Translated by Joana Chaves. Lisbon: Instituto Piaget, 1995. p. 92.

[48] Following Streck, it can be said that solipsistic refers to "an encapsulated consciousness that does not come out of itself when making decisions". This subject is the *Selbstsuchtiger,* "which means selfish, self-sufficient, encapsulated". STRECK, Lenio Luiz. *What is this - I decide according to my conscience?* Vol. I. Porto Alegre: Livraria do Advogado, 2010. p. 56-7. However, we mustn't forget Heidegger's warning: "The fundamental error of solipsism is that, in the midst of *solus ipse,* it forgets to take seriously the fact that every 'I alone' is already, as a being alone, essentially a being-one-with-the-other. Only because the 'I' is already with others can it understand another. HEIDEGGER, Martin. *Introduction to Philosophy.* Translated by Marco Antonio Casanova. Sao Paulo: Martins Fontes, 2009. p. 125-26. Therefore, solipsism is a deception. Anyone who believes that they judge according to their conscience and decide as they wish, and that others are conforming to their position, incurs the serious error of the total impossibility of being alone, of existing.

[49] "The appeal is thus a silent cry. It's not essential to speak out loud, vocal emission is not necessary. It is the sign that the voice of consciousness does not come from outside. It resonates within the being of *Dasein* like an echo from afar. Isn't the silence of the call, the silence of what is far away, an ever more disturbing silence? Because in going forth, the being of *Dasein* recedes, falls behind and remains in oblivion". PASQUA, Herve. *Introduction to Martin Heidegger's Being and Time. Translated by Joana Chaves. Lisbon:* Instituto Piaget, 1995. p. 135-36.

without giving way to curiosity. What is understood by calling in this way is consciousness [50].

But let's go back to the being-in-the-world we were talking about in the first chapter, and consequently to Dasein, because it is fundamental to this analysis of authenticity. Perhaps the best definition of Dasein is to say that Dasein is being-in-the-world [51]. However, this cannot be understood in the sense that Dasein is in the world, like other beings, and as if Dasein were something external or foreign to the world. On the contrary, the world is an existential, a way of being of Dasein. There is no Dasein without the world, just as there is no world without Dasein. At the same time as Dasein's network of references between entities establishes the context through which it is possible to understand the phenomenon of the world, this referential arrangement constitutes Dasein's own world:

> [The whole of everything] that which Dasein understands itself in advance in the mode of referring itself, is precisely that with a view to which the being is previously allowed to appear. The in-what of self-referring understanding, understood as that with a view to which it allows itself to appear to the beings that have the mode of being of the respective condition, is the phenomenon of the world. It is the structure of what Dasein refers to and what constitutes the worldliness of the world. [52]

Therefore

> Worldliness' is an ontological concept that refers to the structure of a constitutive moment of being-in-the-world. Even though being-in-the-world is manifested as an existential determination of Dasein. According to this, worldliness itself is an existential. When we ask about the 'world' from an ontological point of view, we in no way abandon the thematic field of the analysis of Dasein. Ontologically, the 'world' is not a determination of that being which is not essentially Dasein, but a character of Dasein itself [53]

---

[50] HEIDEGGER, Martin. *Sein undZeit*. 19. ed. Tubingen: Max Niemeyer Verlag, 2006. p. 271.

[51] STEIN, Ernildo. *Six studies on "Being and Time"*. 4.ed. Petropolis: Editora Vozes, 2008. p. 42.

[52] HEIDEGGER, Martin. *Sein undZeit*. 19. ed. Tubingen: Max Niemeyer Verlag, 2006. p. 87.

[53] HEIDEGGER, Martin. *Sein undZeit*. 19. ed. Tubingen: Max Niemeyer Verlag, 2006. p. 64.

To understand this better, firstly, we need to know that the concept of the world is ontological, since it concerns Dasein's way of being. Secondly, we need to know the concept of the world. Let's get to it. At first glance, the world appears as a set of objects containing houses, trees, cars, chalk, in short, objects. However, we must be aware that this description remains ontic, and as we pointed out at the beginning of this paragraph, the concept of the world we are referring to is ontological. Therefore, the world is not merely a sum of objects, because these are beings. Entities presuppose the world, but they are not the world. It is not the objects that explain the world, but the world that explains the objects. Nor is it possible to understand the world through objects, but it is possible to understand objects through the world.

To put it another way: an object is simply an object. From the moment that Dasein understands this object as a tool that serves something, Dasein understands this object as a being-for (that is, an existential) and this is a remission. In other words, a remission is the relationship that is made between objects; this "serves for" is what can be understood as a remission. That is, the relationship established between entities. There is a double reference of the utensil: to other utensils and to Dasein.

For it is this way of understanding utensils and creating connections between them that constitutes the world, and that is why the world should not be understood as the sum of entities. The world only becomes the world through Dasein, which is why the world is always the world of Dasein.

When dealing with Dasein as being-in-the-world, Hubert L. Dreyfus clarifies very well the profound relationship that Dasein maintains with the world. This is not merely an ontic relationship, like a subject who relates to objects, but a relationship of mutual belonging, or, more than that, of "dwelling". According to Dreyfus,

> What Heidegger is getting at is a mode of being-in we might call
> "inhabiting". When we inhabit something, it is no longer an object for us

but becomes part of us and pervades our relation to other objects in the world. Both Heidegger and Michael Polanyi call this way of being-in "dwelling". Polanyi points out that we dwell in our language; we feel at home in it and relate to objects and other people through it. Heidegger says the same for the world. Dwelling is Dasein's basic way of being-in-the-world. The relation between me and what I inhabit cannot be understood on the model of the relation between subject and object [54].

Since each Dasein is inserted into a particular facticity, one that is his or her own, he or she will also establish a very particular network of relationships between beings. Again, this relationship is not a mere subjectivism, because the being with whom this (unique) relationship will be established is external to Dasein, which, according to Heidegger, rules out subjectivity.

The network of relationships between entities essentially refers to Dasein.

Since Dasein exists as a possibility of being, and every projection is based on each Dasein's understanding of the world, it is within these possibilities that the system of references that make up Dasein's world originates. To explain: by projecting itself as a possibility, Dasein has created a network of relationships between entities. As every entity "serves a purpose", Dasein plans the use of each tool it will need to realize its initial project.

Everything depends on Dasein's understanding of the world. Thus, in the focus listed here, it can be said that the judge also follows his understanding of the world and of the Law (which is part of the world, and therefore cannot be a solipsistic understanding) in order to make his decision. In this way, every decision will be circumscribed within the limits of the judge's power of understanding. After all, how can he decide what he hasn't already understood?

---

[54] DREYFUS, Hubert L. *Being-in-the-World: a commentary on Heidegger's Being and Time, Division I.* Cambridge, Massachusetts/London/England: The MIT Press, 1991. p. 45. Free translation: "What Heidegger wants to affirm is a mode of being-in that we can call 'inhabiting'. When we inhabit something, it is no longer an object for us but becomes part of us and penetrates our relationship with other objects in the world. Both Heidegger and Michael Polanyi call this form of being-in "dwelling". Polanyi points out that we dwell in our language; we feel at home in it and relate to objects and other people through it. Heidegger says the same for the world. Dwelling is Dasein's basic way of being-in-the-world. The relationship between me and what I inhabit cannot be understood in the way of the relationship between subject and object".

Everything that Dasein does (which is to assume modes of being) takes place in the world. But not as a subject that is inserted in the midst of beings (that would be a subject-object perception). In the very ontological constitution of Dasein, it is already being-in-the-world. It's not geographical, it's a co-pertaining between Dasein and the world. Dasein shapes the world through its way of being.

William Richardson makes points that are very helpful to our approach.

> Langed between beings, man is open to his Being and yet finds himself hindered by his finitude. The privileged experience through which man discovers the unity of the self is anxiety. Anxiety is a special form of ontological disposition, an affective and non-rational affinity within us. It is different from fear, because fear is always an apprehensive reaction to something - like the dentist's drill. But in anxiety, the self is not anxious about something, but about nothing, in particular, about Nothing! At that moment, things that have a "where" around them seem to escape our grasp, to lose their meaning. We no longer feel at ease among them. We are alienated from them; we are also alienated from "everyone else", from the in-crowd, with everything it says and does. We discover that there is another dimension to life than the everyday one, a new horizon of which we are not usually aware, but within which and for which we truly exist, whether we call this horizon simply Nothingness, the World or even Being itself. Through the phenomenon of anxiety, therefore, the self becomes aware of itself as a unified whole - related to the beings within the World, but open to Being, to the World as such - aware, too, of the possibility of accepting the fact that this is what it is (finite transcendence) or of evading the truth by refusing to know anything except what the crowd knows. In other words, the phenomenon of anxiety gives man the possibility of choosing between being authentic or not [55].

This quote must necessarily be accompanied by a clarification. The Nothingness of Heideggerian philosophy cannot be confused with the Nothingness thought of by the Greeks, or the Nothingness of the Christian tradition. This Nothing to which William refers is a Nothing that veils being, or rather, it is "the veil of being".[56]. There are no nihilisms or pessimisms. It is in a transcendental dimension, nothingness is simply non-being.

Since we've talked about ontology, and ontology is part of metaphysics,

---

[55] WILLIAM, J. Richardson. Humanism and Existential Psychology. IN: GREENING, Thomas C. (Org.) *Existential-Humanist Psychology.* Translated by Eduardo de Almeida. Rio de Janeiro: Zahar Editores, 1975, p. 177-78. One observation is important: because of the translation, where William mentions anxiety, it should be understood in the same sense as anguish.

[56] HEIDEGGER, Martin. *Conferences and philosophical writings.* Translated by Vergilio Ferreira. São Paulo: Victor Civita, 1973 (Os Pensadores, XLV). p. 228.

it seems pertinent at this point to talk a little about metaphysics. Starting from a semantic conception, the particle *meta* means beyond, after, and, *physics* establishes a relationship with the notion of physical experience. In other words, it means beyond physics, or "the things that are beyond physics".[57].

Metaphysics was designed as a science by Aristotle and is the first science, in the sense that it provides all the others with a common foundation. That is to say: metaphysics provides the first principles, which serve as the foundation for all sciences.

In history, following the writings of Streck , [58]we say that metaphysics has presented itself in three fundamental forms, which must essentially be identified and analyzed differently:

1) Theology: metaphysics is the science of what lies beyond experience. Here, the object of metaphysics is the highest and most perfect being, on which all other beings and things in the world depend. It is what Aristotle calls "something eternal, immovable and separate".

2) Ontology: metaphysics is the study of the fundamental characteristics of being. It is also a primary science, which establishes the fundamental principles that condition the validity of all other principles.

3) Gnosiology: is the branch of metaphysics that deals with knowledge, especially as a theory of knowledge. One of its main exponents was Kant, who sought to explain the way in which man is capable of knowing, and to explain the limits of this capacity. This form of metaphysics studies the forms that condition human thought and also condition all of science.

Stein points out that metaphysics began in antiquity with the distinction between essence *(Essentia)* and existence *(Existentia).* It was precisely in this

---

[57] MORA, Jose Ferrater. Metaphysics. IN: *Dicionario de Filosofia.* Sao Paulo: Martins Fontes, 1988. p. 467.

[58] STRECK, Lenio Luiz. *Truth and Consensus: Constitution, Hermeneutics and Discursive Theories.* 4.ed. Sao Paulo: Saraiva, 2011. p. 346-47.

distinction that Being was veiled. Heidegger will reformulate this relationship and give it a new meaning.

We can point to other well-known philosophers who subsequently followed this new relationship proposed by Heidegger - at least partially - as did Sartre, who copied this "first part" of the inversion but did not adopt Heidegger's new reading of meaning. Thus, Sartre kept to the previous view, without realizing the difference between Being and being, working on the subject as consciousness (without equivalents to Being and being). In fact, Sartre will invert the order, as Heidegger did, but he will continue to look for the essence in things. This is the big difference between Heidegger and Sartre: for Heidegger, there is no essence in advance, the essence is in the existence of Dasein. Heidegger also analyzes other philosophers, such as Descartes, criticizing the *cogito* in particular, accusing it of being the greatest sign of the oblivion of Being. Why? Because Descartes maintained that, based on reason, the subject, even in isolation from the world, could arrive at the truth - see the similarity that our solipsistic judge of today has with this thought[59]. In other words, it's a solipsistic subject who doesn't need the outside world to know the world. Nothing outside of it matters to him. With this, consciousness is born and with it, in this form, the subject vs. object schema. A subject that subjects an object, precisely the point that Heidegger set out to overcome. For him, consciousness and Being cannot be born from consciousness (this link, this birth is metaphysics because it works exclusively with concepts). In this vein, Heidegger also criticizes Kant (Subject - Object and a priori), Hegel, Nietzsche and countless other renowned philosophers, with the same argument: they have all forgotten Being.

Specifically, metaphysics deals with themes such as God, soul, freedom, notions that have taken on the most varied concepts in the history of

---

[59] See STRECK, Lenio Luiz. *What is this - I decide according to my conscience?* Vol. I. Porto Alegre: Livraria do Advogado, 2010.

philosophy, depending on each philosopher. In a passage from the book Introduction to Philosophy, Heidegger says that metaphysics is "knowledge of being as such in its totality, knowledge of being in general, that is, in concepts; and this means at the same time: from concepts and exclusively from concepts".[60].

This is exactly the criticism that is made. Metaphysics thinks of being as being and, in questioning this being as being, metaphysics no longer turns to Being, but remains close to being. As a result, metaphysics began to treat being as if it were Being. "Being is not thought in its unveiling essence, that is, in its truth"[61].

This is because metaphysics is, by its very essence, excluded from the experience of Being. By representing being as being, metaphysics does not have the capacity to unveil what is veiled in the manifestation of being - and I don't need to tell you again how important this is. Therefore, traditional metaphysics has shown that it does not have the capacity to understand that being differs from Being. "Metaphysics thinks about being and dwells on being; by equating being with being, it quantifies being through objectifying thought"[62]. However, there is no split between Being and being, they are a unity - albeit distinct - but they need different paths to be unveiled. This is why Heidegger takes the beginning of metaphysics as his starting point, and thinks of Being as history.

In this sense, Ernildo Stein will say: "Heidegger sets out to think of Being as history, through the step back to the essence of metaphysics, which is hidden in its comego".[63]. The Gaucho philosopher continues: "Metaphysics,

[60] HEIDEGGER, Martin. *Introduction to Philosophy.* Translated by Marco Antonio Casanova. Sao Paulo: Martins Fontes, 2009. p. 271.

[61] HEIDEGGER, Martin. Conferences and philosophical writings. Translated by Vergilio Ferreira. São Paulo: Victor Civita, 1973. (Os Pensadores, XLV). p. 253.

[62] STRECK, Lenio Luiz. Truth and Consensus: Constitution, Hermeneutics and Discursive Theories. 4.ed. Sao Paulo: Saraiva, 2011. p. 215.

[63] STEIN, Ernildo. *Introduction to the thought of Martin Heidegger.* Porto Alegre: EDIPUCRS, 2002.

as the history of Being, is the history of its forgetfulness. This forgetting is the very essence of metaphysics. Metaphysics no longer has access to itself".[64].

For Heidegger, the history of metaphysics is the history of the forgetting of Being, and each historical moment is distinguished by its own mode of representation: "every philosophy is the expression of a historical vision of Being".[65]. It is the translation of the particular way in which man interprets himself as Being-in-the-world.

This also means that metaphysics has defined the truth in each historical moment, which is nothing more than the explanation of the being in each period, and of a certain conception of truth, transmitted by metaphysics itself.

It should be emphasized, however, that Heidegger does not seek to deny metaphysics (which is why we give it so much prominence in the search for the answer to the judge's authenticity), nor does he propose its extinction. On the contrary,

Heidegger proposes a new beginning, starting not from being, but from Being as the foundation of being. For this reason, in his writings entitled *The End of Philosophy and the Task of Thought*[66]he states:

> Philosophy and metaphysics. Metaphysics thinks of being in its totality - the world, man, God - from the point of view of being, from the point of view of the reciprocal imbrication of being and being. Metaphysics thinks of being as being in the manner of the founding representation (...). Being as a foundation brings being to its proper presentness. The foundation manifests itself as being present. Its present consists in producing for the present each being that presents itself in its own particular way[67] .

---

p. 91-2.

[64] STEIN, Ernildo. *Introduction to the thought of Martin Heidegger.* Porto Alegre: EDIPUCRS, 2002. p. 91-2.

[65] RESWEBER, Jean-Paul. *The thought of Martin Hiedegger.* Translated by Joao Agostinho A. Santos. Coimbra: Livraria Almedina, 1979. p. 75.

[66] HEIDEGGER, Martin. *Conferences and philosophical writings.* Translated by Vergilio Ferreira. Sao Paulo: Victor Civita, 1973. (Os Pensadores, XLV). p. 269.

[67] HEIDEGGER, Martin. *Conferences and philosophical writings.* Translated by Vergilio Ferreira.

Being can only be thought of in its totality on the basis of its being, since it is on account of its being that being presents itself in its own particular way. That is to say: since being presents itself - makes itself present - together with Dasein always being, in a certain particular way, it is from this being that a new metaphysics must be constructed. It is in this sense that Heidegger promotes what he calls the "overcoming of metaphysics", in which overcoming does not mean rejecting, but returning to the foundation of metaphysics, and starting again, but this time from the ontological difference, which is the necessary recognition of the difference between Being and being.

While limited to the subject-object relationship, metaphysics sought to explain the being of entities by referring to other entities. As a result, there was the impasse of returning to infinity. To resolve this, we need a framework in which we can "stop" questioning. For example, in Kelsen, we have the fundamental norm; in Aristotle, the immovable engine; for the thinkers of the Middle Ages, there was the figure of God who took on this function. Metaphysics based a statement about an entity on another statement about an entity. In other words, it is the foundation of an entity in another entity, and this tells us nothing about it or its Being.

This is one of the problems that Heidegger tries to solve with the distinction between Being and being. With the understanding of Being, we have an ante-enunciative, ante-predicative condition, that is, a pre-comprehension that gives us access to meaning about beings.

Dasein is the place where the difference between Being and being is sustained, and its capacity for pre-understanding allows it to overcome the subject-object schema, because it already has an understanding of Being. He already knows, even if he doesn't, that Being is one thing and being another.

That's why it's necessary to overcome metaphysics in order to study Being. This failure to overcome (known or not) that we still see today in the

---

Sao Paulo: Victor Civita, 1973. (Os Pensadores, XLV). p. 269.

Judiciary, at various times, is what is costing us dearly today, mainly because, for inexplicable reasons, legal *practitioners* believe they are immune to the events and revolutions that have taken place in philosophy, even though philosophy is the condition of possibility for understanding law. Or, as Streck puts it in his questioning way: "why would law be 'shielded' from the influences of this paradigmatic revolution?"[68]Is it possible to conceive of law in isolation from philosophy?

---

[68] STRECK, Lenio Luiz. What is this - I decide according to my conscience? Vol. I. Porto Alegre: Livraria do Advogado, 2010. p. 70.

CHAPTER III

How judging on the basis of other decisions masks metaphysics and costs constitutional jurisdiction dearly: between (in)authenticity and judicial (ir)responsibilities

But what is this (ir)responsibility that we deal with throughout this work? A responsibility referred to as non-procedural, non-administrative because of the position, but a responsibility in Heideggerian hermeneutic terms?

Right. When this responsibility of the judge, of the decision-maker, is questioned, it is in the sense of the need for him not to close himself off from the world, preventing him from unveiling the meaning of things, of the judgments he makes, by being merely inauthentic. This is because the inauthentic is "just anyone" who has a mistaken view of themselves, and someone who chooses to live like this, or rather, who allows themselves to be like this, cannot be in the position of decision-maker. The decision to occupy this kind of position should make the struggle to remain inauthentic impossible.

Adalberto Hommerding - in the context of analyzing the former paragraph 3 of art. 515 of the CPC - made the right points in this regard. Even with the change in procedural legislation that came into force in 2016, his comments should be brought into our discussion, since, although some provisions of the rule have been changed, its essence (although now in other articles) remains the same. Hommerding told us:

> Obviously, we are not saying that the judge will behave in such a way as not to judge the merits. Of course, the concern that accompanies - or, rather, should accompany - all judges is to provide adequate judicial protection. However, one cannot fail to mention the issue of the judge's responsibility in relation to the substance of the case, even if this is a matter of law. This is because the subject under discussion, in addition to

That's why we're arguing here that judges can't make decisions solely on the basis of other decisions they've already made. Nor should they "justify" their decisions solely on the basis of Supreme Court rulings (not even binding ones). Reproducing what has already been done, what everyone does, is metaphysical. Applying a ready-made decision to a case is pure metaphysics (the kind already surpassed by Heidegger). The decision of that case only exists in the authenticity of the person who is seeking the meaning of that case. There is only one being-in-the-world of the situation under judgment. This does not imply that decisions should be unique and isolated, nor is this the way.

That's why hermeneutics is also a way of looking at the problem of judicial decision-making and, in this context, the question of the responsibility of judges in their decisions. It's worth remembering that hermeneutic phenomenology differs completely from metaphysics. You could say that metaphysics replaces everything with a statement (an entity), without realizing the space in which it takes place (and this space is Being). Hermeneutic phenomenology seeks to interpret the dimension it achieves as an understanding of Being. This understanding is Dasein's way of Being, which is always linked to a way of understanding that anticipates the being of the entities about which it makes its statements. Thus, hermeneutics is a mode of anticipatory understanding. Understanding is the condition of possibility for every statement about being, it is hermeneutics.

---

* HOMMERDING, Adalberto Narciso. Paragraph 3 of Article 515 of the Civil Procedure Code: an analysis in the light of the hermeneutic philosophy (or philosophical hermeneutics) of Heidegger and Gadamer. IN: *Revista da AJURIS/Associaqao dos Juizes do Rio Grande do Sul* - v. 30, n. 91. Porto Alegre: AJURIS, Sep. 2003. p. 19.

being and assume themselves to be inescapably thrown into existence. In this way, hermeneutics is a way in which the human being's way of being is revealed in the understanding that relates him to being and to himself simultaneously (...). The something as something apophatic refers to the mode of relation of the being in the statement, while the hermeneutic is the mode of anticipatory understanding. (...). With this double structure, the philosopher introduces the mode of circular "grounding" into philosophy and replaces the sensible-suppressible distinction and the subject-object schema, which were the basis of the grounding model of metaphysics [70].

Following this line of reasoning, it can be said that Heidegger introduced a mode of circular reasoning that broke with the search for reasoning in the infinite, overcoming the theories of consciousness. Having overcome the theories of consciousness many years ago, and living in a democracy, there is no longer anything to justify a judge deciding as he sees fit, as "his feeling" "authorizes" him. And this form of decision can be rejected by different ways of looking at the issue, whether through Systems Theory (as we have already done), or through Heideggerian theory and so many other theories of Philosophy, Sociology and Politics.

With this observation, we see that Heidegger established "the hermeneutic circle, the understanding of being by the being-there that understands itself in its own being, as a place to sustain the ontological difference between being and being".[71]. This is the path taken by a new paradigm that overcomes exactly what is still insistently observed today in judicial decisions.

But in order to verify the depth of these questions, it seems necessary to discuss a little more about understanding and interpretation in Heidegger.

Understanding is an existential, in other words, a way of Being of Dasein, forming part of the constitutive structure of this Dasein. There is only Dasein within an understanding. Dasein is what it projects and only projects

---

[70]   STEIN, Ernildo. *Thinking and making mistakes: an adjustment with Heidegger.* Ijuí: Editora UNUJUI, 2011. p. 36-7.

[71]   STEIN, Ernildo. *Thinking and making mistakes: an adjustment with Heidegger.* Ijuí: Editora UNUJUI, 2011. p. 38.

into what it understands (there is a relationship of circularity).

Understanding existentially includes Dasein's way of being as Being-Power. The link between Dasein and understanding is possibility.

> The whole from which being-itself is understood, the world, is not a system of ontological propositions hovering freely in the air. On the contrary, to understand oneself means to exist by virtue of oneself, and that means to be in itself exposed to being. The world delivers the being-there to the being, exposing it to the necessity of confrontation with the being that it is not and with itself. The being-there is given to the being, and not just because the being is subsistent in itself. On the contrary, surrender is an inherent determination of being-in-the-world as such[72].

In fact, Dasein's understanding of the world cannot be confused with an encounter with objects, in an apophantic way, but it is a surrender in which the being-there will transcend, will surpass it, not from a choice of this or that, but in the totality of beings.

Take a look at Heidegger's considerations:

> In the statement "that chalk is white", we, the enunciators, don't go through that relational context; we don't first turn to one or two representations which we then link in order to relate to that white chalk through that representational link. On the contrary, everything is completely different: before the proposition is enunciated, we are already immediately related to the thing itself, to the white chalk, but not in such a way that we would only have a "representation" of that chalk in our soul. In making the enunciation, we are already standing next to the chalk. We are already together with the chalk itself, since it is simply this subsistent thing. When we enunciate, we are aiming directly at the chalk itself beforehand. We, the subjects, relate directly to this entity (chalk) itself; we are close to it. Our, the subject's, relationship with the object is a direct "being next to" the chalk [73].

To this example, we can add our previous considerations, adding language. When we talked about chalk earlier, we already had an understanding of what chalk is, without having to see it as you read this text and I write it. In fact, this understanding may not be exactly the same for everyone, as some may think of chalk for scratching clothes and others of

---

[72] HEIDEGGER, Martin. *Introduction to Philosophy*. Translated by Marco Antonio Casanova. Sao Paulo: Martins Fontes, 2009. p. 349-350.

[73] HEIDEGGER, Martin. *Introduction to Philosophy*. Translated by Marco Antonio Casanova. Sao Paulo: Martins Fontes, 2009. p.68-9.

chalk for writing on a blackboard. Now, if I choose to speak аптека[74]not all readers are able to know, to understand what is being said (not just the spelling); they may have imagined something, but not known for sure what it was. That's why comprehension, this being-together-with, will be linked to language (which, as we've just seen, can sometimes be limited by the way it is used, whether written or spoken). If you don't understand, if you don't have language, you can't reach Being. That's why language is not a third thing between the subject and the object, it constitutes Dasein. "We never start from the sound of the word; a spoken proposition is always more"[75]. You can't say anything about chalk if it isn't through language (and no legal decisions would be or have been made without language); there is a relationship of totality between entities and Dasein. "This whole is the primary and most original element, and only against its background is it possible to take the parts as such and in their relations"[76]You can touch the chalk, you can rub it between your hands, but that won't make you understand it: understanding comes through language[77].

It turns out that both the world of Dasein and Dasein itself depend on how Dasein understands the world and itself. When Dasein projects itself, this act of projecting itself reveals Dasein's understanding of the world and of itself. As the possibilities of projecting oneself are always infinite, and all of them are always possibilities, Dasein is characterized as a possibility of being

---

[74] аптека is the Russian word for pharmacy. Therefore, when considering it in this explanation, you have to think about how it sounds when pronounced. That's why language is so important when it comes to understanding and interpretation. Sometimes, even the choice of language interferes with communication. What's more, you have to remember that every time something is said, a selection has been made of various other things that have not been said (unspoken), which also, to a certain extent, has to be taken into account when understanding.

[75] HEIDEGGER, Martin. *Introduction to Philosophy.* Translated by Marco Antonio Casanova. Sao Paulo: Martins Fontes, 2009. p. 63.

[76] HEIDEGGER, Martin. *Introduction to Philosophy.* Translated by Marco Antonio Casanova. Sao Paulo: Martins Fontes, 2009. p. 63.

[77] Language is so important that Heidegger calls it "The House of Being". This is a figurative, poetic expression to explain that one cannot reach Being unless through language.

within its understanding. Therefore, understanding and projecting. When making a decision, for example, although the number of possibilities is infinitely smaller, the judge needs to project the arguments he intends to use in this decision, the decision to be made and how to justify it. To do this, however, they first need to understand their way of being, their power-to-be, but they also need language. Thus, after understanding the case, and seeing its uniqueness, he will be able to project and thus interpret in order to make sense of it. Only after the world has been understood can it be interpreted.

The problem is that the world has always been understood. And inauthenticity has always been a way of understanding the world. However, inauthenticity brings about an inadequate understanding of Being. Moreover, running away from the impersonal is its very condition for Being. Inauthenticity is an alienation, it fails to mirror the singularity that characterizes Dasein.

The authentic way of being opens the way to new meanings. Because of their uniqueness, meanings are constructed in each case. This implies a change in the way we understand the world and authenticity represents a richer and more complete form of participation in the public context. According to Guignon,

> Heidegger states that authenticity "does not separate Dasein from its world"; the world "does not become other in its content, nor is the circulated Other replaced by a new one" (SZ 344). In fact, since our own life stories are inseparable from the broader text of a world we share, authenticity can be nothing more than a fuller and richer form of participation in the public context.[78]

Interpretation requires something to be given, and this something needs to be understood in order to be interpreted. In other words, as Streck reminds

---

[78] GUIGNON, Charles. *Authenticity, moral values and psychotherapy* IN: The Cambridge Companion To Heidegger. New York: Cambridge University Press, 1993. p. 228.

us, first you understand because you already have a pre-understanding and then you interpret, using language, but without any compromise[79].

So, since the entity has no meaning in itself, and only what can be understood by Dasein has meaning, it can be said that meaning is given to the world and to entities by Dasein. Meaning is linked to Dasein's Being and Dasein gives meaning to the world based on its understanding of the world.

To put it more succinctly: the purpose for which a hammer is used depends on Dasein's understanding of the being hammer and the relationship that Dasein has with the objects that can be hammered. Here we have: a) Dasein's understanding of the hammer and its relationship to other beings; b) the meaning that Dasein has attributed to the hammer as an entity that has a purpose.

> Those who know how to use a tool don't turn it into an object, but work with it. Likewise, understanding, which allows the pre-sentient to know himself in his being and in his world, is not a behavior related to certain objects of knowledge, but his own being-in-the-world.[80]

So, as understanding is part of Dasein, since it doesn't exist Dasein outside of an understanding, Dasein is also linked to the Meaning it attributes to beings and the world. In a final word: Dasein, Meaning, Understanding and Language are always interconnected.

It is important to emphasize that, in the line we have been taking here, more than just giving reasons for a decision, it is necessary to justify the reasons that led to that decision. In a hermeneutic sense, it can be said that it is necessary to explain what has been understood. Understanding is the condition for interpreting, and interpreting is giving meaning. In order to effectively externalize a meaning, it is imperative to give reasons for it. The explication of this understanding, in addition to making the decision authentic,

---

STRECK, Lenio Luiz. Truth and Consensus: Constitution, Hermeneutics and Discursive Theories. 4.ed. Sao Paulo: Saraiva, 2011. p. 285.

GADAMER, Hans-Georg. *Truth and Method II: Supplements and Index.* Translated by Enio Paulo Gaichini 2. ed. Braganga Paulista: Editora Universitaria Sao Francisco; Petropolis: Editora Vozes, 2004. p. 382.

in Heideggerian philosophical terms, will also avoid arbitrariness[81].

> That being the case - we say - the law expert has to be "distressed" in the face of the concrete case, he has to participate in its history in "care", and with an attentive eye on the thing, with an eye on the phenomenon, on the fact. It cannot cling to "abstractions" such as "law in theory" (as if validity were "given" in advance) or "conceptualisms". Rather, it must assume itself as (one of) the interpreter(s) of (and in) the Law, and with the responsibilities that this entails[82].

In this discussion about authenticity and responsibility, it seems that there are everyday situations that at some point present themselves in terms of court decisions.

In Brazil, it has become common practice for decision-makers to believe that their decisions are following "the chain" of discourse and are therefore "grounded" solely on the basis of quotes from other judgments, or even by using copies of sentences (which are stored in the Sentence Bank) from other colleagues who have already decided cases with some similarity. Certainly, this has a great deal to do with the lack of understanding of philosophy and, more specifically, of Ronald Dworkin in Brazil (but that's a subject for another time).

However, decisions made in this way not only violate democratic precepts, but are also irresponsible from a hermeneutic point of view and lack a rationale. Giving reasons is not a matter of quoting a sentence. A "I'm ruling this way because the Court has already ruled this way", "In this sense", is not a statement of reasons. Although it seems obvious, it has to be said: quoting articles of law at random is not a statement of reasons either. Furthermore, "if I have accepted the arguments of one party, it is obvious that I have rejected those of the other, and I do not need to justify this obviousness", is even more

---

[81] Here we will not distinguish between arbitrariness, discretion and the other terms that have emerged in recent years to deal with this judicial stance. For an in-depth study of the subject, we suggest TASSINARI, Clarissa. *Jurisdiction and Judicial Activism: the limits of judicial action.* Porto Alegre: Livraria do Advogado, 2013.

[82] MOTTA, Francisco Jose Borges. *Levando o Direito a Serio: uma critica hermeneutica ao protagonismo judicial.* 2. ed. Porto Alegre: Livraria do Advogado, 2012. p. 119-120.

erroneous, legally, constitutionally and hermeneutically.

This is not to say that it is enough for the judge to mention these provisions, saying "I decided this way because of art. x, of Law y". No, this would not be a hermeneutically correct reasoning either. However, exempting the judge from explaining everything - including the legal provisions - that served as the basis for his decision is an affront to art. 93, IX of the FC [83].

What needs to be said is: why should this article of law be used in this case? Why can this case law, this summary, the judgment previously handed down, be elements that serve as arguments to decide this specific case? Even "mass actions" can have their peculiarities, and if they don't (i.e. this needs to be analyzed on a case-by-case basis), this absence needs to be stated. There is no obviousness in terms of judicial argumentation. The traditional phrase we hear from judges when we question them, "it's obvious that if I used this article, this ementa, it's because it fits the case", "it's obvious that if I used the same decision I've used in other contract reviews, it's because they're the same", doesn't contain any obviousness, and only shows their lack of understanding of the social role they've decided to play. Phrases like that sound more like disrespect for the citizen.

In our view, one example (of the many we could give in this book) of a totally irresponsible decision is found in first-degree judgment number 001/2.05.0706814-0 of the Porto Alegre District Court. When analyzing whether or not to accept a complaint offered by the Public Prosecutor's Office, the first instance judge, in a totally inauthentic way, uses only another decision as a decisive argument. As can be seen in Streck's analysis: "Theft. Rejection of the complaint. Principle of insignificance. Case that characterizes the crime of bagatelle, giving rise to the application of the principle of insignificance. Appeal dismissed". Nothing more was said[84].

---

[83] LUIZ, Fernando Vieira. *Teoria da Decisao Judicial: dos paradigmas de Ricardo Lorenzetti a resposta adequada a Constituigao de Lenio Streck.* Porto Alegre: Livraria do Advogado, 2011. p. 58.
[84] STRECK, Lenio Luiz. *Truth and Consensus: Constitution, Hermeneutics and Discursive*

This is a clear example of what we see every day in the Brazilian judiciary. In addition to being an affront to the law, what we have is that no meaning has been revealed in this decision, there is no explanation of what is understood in the specific case. Why should insignificance be recognized in this specific case? What is the relationship between the case in which this ementa originated and the case being analyzed that authorizes the use of the judgment, so that it can form part of the reasoning behind the decision that puts an end to that process? What happened in the specific case that makes this previous decision (which must also be substantiated in procedural terms, since it is a judgment rejecting a complaint) valuable enough to be the only argument in the decision? We know nothing, because nothing has been said and, hermeneutically, nothing has been decided.

What exists today is just a model of irresponsible repetition. After an appeal was lodged by the Public Prosecutor's Office, the decision was completely overturned,

in these terms.

> The ministerial claim deserves to prosper, I explain.
> First of all, it is worth remembering that this judicial unit adheres to the concept of minimum and subsidized criminal law, and not infrequently applies the principle of insignificance to certain crimes. However, the recognition of the crime of bagatelle and, consequently, the inappropriateness of criminal intervention in such cases is conditioned not only by the derisory nature of the goods involved, but also by the conditions surrounding the victim and the circumstances in which the unlawful acts occur. Thus, although tangentially, the individual situation of the victim, and even that of the perpetrator, is taken into account.
> Thus, we see here a willingness to recover the complexity that surrounds the crime, which for too long has been vilified by the criminal justice system which, by monopolizing it, removes from it the vitalizing and humanizing characters expressed in the singularities and desires of the parties.
> In this sense, in particular, it must be taken into account that, although the goods stolen amounted to the derisory sum of R$100.00 (fl. 25), the crime was perpetrated in competition with agents, was marked by the boldness of the agents who broke into the victim's home and, furthermore, the victim was assaulted by the accused when she tried to

---

Theories.

4.ed. Sao Paulo: Saraiva, 2011. p. 279.

restrain him in order to retrieve her belongings.
Therefore, exceptionally, I believe that the small value of the stolen goods is irrelevant to the characterization of bagatelle, due to the other elements surrounding the criminal conduct, which undoubtedly challenge the intervention of the criminal justice system.
In view of the above, I vote in favor of granting the ministerial appeal, so that the monocratic decision may be reversed and the complaint received, with the case proceeding[85] .

It should be noted that this decision says more than the existence of a violation of the Federal Constitution, more than the occurrence of an affront to the right of the citizen (and everyone, not just those directly involved) to a reasoned response. This decision shows an attachment to classical metaphysics and a validity, via hermeneutics, that is highly questionable.

Of course, we're not arguing that every case has to be decided from scratch. There is no zero degree of meaning in the matrix adopted here. This is perhaps one of the necessary orthodoxies mentioned in the first lines of this paper. However, a decision that wants to use jurisprudence must necessarily give reasons for the decision added to its opinion and, more than that, explain the peculiar situations of the case under analysis with the case analyzed when the cited jurisprudence was drawn up. In the same way, it is not acceptable for each judge to decide as they wish, breaking with the previous decisions of the lower court. In other words:

Jurisprudence does not simply mean a set of judged cases. An isolated case that has "broken" the sequence of decisions and has not been followed is likely to have been the result of an arbitrary decision; likewise, breaking the sequence without giving reasons, simply by saying "in this case I do not follow the case law", has "zero" hermeneutical validity[86] .

Within this item "I decide like this because it has already been decided

---

Criminal Appeal No. 70012342515, judged on January 25, 2006, by the Fifth Criminal Chamber of the Court of Justice of the State of Rio Grande do Sul. It should be noted that, although the decision was reformed, the most serious fact is that the Court did not mention anything about the lack of grounds for the decision.

STRECK, Lenio Luiz. *Truth and Consensus: Constitution, Hermeneutics and Discursive Theories*. 4.ed. Sao Paulo: Saraiva, 2011. p. 551.

like this", in which it is understood that there is a high probability that a judge will decide in an inauthentic way, another promoter of this decisional irresponsibility can be found in the Sentence Bank[87]. First set up by the Corregedoria Geral de Justiga of the State Court of Mato Grosso, it is now present in several Brazilian states, either under this name or even through folders in sectorial emails.[88]In a nutshell, it can be said that the purpose of this tool is to keep a number of court decisions handed down by judges, which are made available to other colleagues so that they can be reused in "identical cases", similar cases, or any other criterion that is deemed interesting, in order to speed up the judicial process at the time of the decision.

At first, it could be a good tool, as it would allow judges to discuss the peculiarities of their cases, their mass actions, for example, in order to find out what causes so many contract reviews in Rio Grande do Sul, what arguments appear in their actions claiming the granting of experimental treatments and medicines.[89]. However, this is not the case and, in many states, this was not even the objective. The objective was clear. Do you have a case that you don't know how to decide? See if another colleague has already ruled and copy their decision. Have you received a flood of mass actions that have already been decided by other colleagues? Copy the decision![90]

Now, a situation in which this happens makes it clear that the judge is being inauthentic, is complacent and is just repeating what others have already done. There can certainly be an attraction in this possibility, but it is at this point that, as the person empowered to decide, the judge cannot allow

---

[87] STRECK, Lenio Luiz. *Truth and Consensus: Constitution, Hermeneutics and Discursive Theories.* 4.ed. Sao Paulo: Saraiva, 2011. p. 254.

[88] The author knows this not only from her research, but also from having had access to them during her time working in the Judiciary, as well as from observing how they are perceived within the institution.

[89] On this subject see: WEBBER, Suelen. *Decision, Risk and Health: the paradox of judicial decision in the face of requests for experimental medicines.* Curitiba: Jurua, 2013.

[90] It should be noted that not all judges act in this way, although this is the perception of the majority.

himself to fall into the inauthentic mode. He can be inauthentic in his personal choices, his day-to-day choices, but in the position of judge, as mentioned above, there is no hermeneutic possibility.

> That's why Heidegger says that, in this comparison of itself with everything, which is tranquil and understands everything, *Dasein* leads to alienation in which its most proper power-being is concealed. The being-in-the-world of decadence is thus tempting and reassuring, in other words, alienating [91].

To think that it is possible for a judge to reuse the decisions of other judges in identical cases, without making his own analysis and his own specific reasoning for the case he is analyzing, is a tempting convenience that corrupts judicial service. The inauthenticity here is blatant, insofar as, although it cannot be denied that there are equal cases - with equal petitions, equal documents, without particularities - and therefore it would be contradictory for the decisions to be different, attention is drawn to the fact that it is not only the final result that matters, but what precedes it, what leads to that decision. Even from a Gadamerian or Dworkinian perspective, it is unlikely that the exact terms of one judge's reasoning will be the same as another. It's possible for the same judge to rule on several of the same cases in the same way on the same grounds - as long as they are explained in the grounds of the decision - but it's unlikely that different judges would produce exactly the same grounds for the cases they analyze separately. To admit this (and to structure and operationalize it, as has been done) is to "authorize" an alienation of the magistrate. It is in this alienation that the judge loses his responsibility as a judge. A decision like this puts the entire system of law in crisis and, over time, contingently, democracy itself.

The judge, who is the one who decides and not the one who chooses,

---

[91] HOMMERDING, Adalberto Narciso. Paragraph 3 of Article 515 of the Civil Procedure Code: an analysis in the light of the hermeneutic philosophy (or philosophical hermeneutics) of Heidegger and Gadamer. IN: *Revista da AJURIS/Associagao dos Juizes do Rio Grande do Sul* - v. 30, n. 91. Porto Alegre: AJURIS, Sep. 2003. p. 21.

cannot fall into this trap. The trap consists in the fact that choosing is linked to a practical reason, and can be full of solipsism, because "I" choose. Deciding requires responsibility, it doesn't depend on "me" and what "I" think. Decision carries the need to move away from these paradigms.

The philosopher Zelijko Loparic, with regard to the need to decide, says that human beings always have two possibilities, which are basically to decide by repetition, a monotonous decision, a decision of decay, or to effectively take on the "reins" of the decision and choose between the existing possibilities, with the possibility of modifying behavior. As beings endowed with reason, there is no possibility of remaining in decay, in inertia.

> Before the distinction between reason and unreason, the choice to choose implies that at no time can we surrender to the inertia of everyday life and tradition. What's more, the voice of a responsible conscience, properly understood, calls us to the second path, to the choice of the choice. (...) The second, more difficult path may *not* be chosen and may even be passed over in favor of the first. But its non-choice implies a guilt/debt towards our 'most proper', 'structural' possibility of transcendence, which, as such, cannot be erased by any historicism. The path of repeating the past is, in essence, just a flight into the past, motivated by the rejection of the relationship with the future, a relationship that is *an a priori* part of the circular structure of the human being, constitutes the very self and always also includes responsibility for the choices made or to be made. It is therefore impossible to reconstruct fatalism within the hermeneutic circle as thought by Heidegger. (...) When we listen to the voice of consciousness, we take on the *original responsibility of* being the horizon on which the meaning of the presence of all beings is decided, as well as the meaning of our concrete projects. In other words, the responsibility for maintaining the openness of the manifestation of beings, transmitted by the voice, unfolds into *two tasks,* an ontological one, towards the different senses of being, and an ontic one, towards our way of acting [92].

And this is exactly what happens when decisions are repeated. Mere repetition for repetition's sake leads to inauthenticity, to entification, to a return to metaphysics. Law, even if it were possible to delude oneself that it is immune to the changes that have occurred in philosophy (especially the linguistic turn and the ontological turn), needs the new, it needs evolution, and

---

[92] LOPARIC, Zelijko. *On responsibility.* Porto Alegre: EDIPUCRS, 2003. p. 117-19.

the new is only possible through reasoned production that brings something legitimately different. This is also the role of the judge, and contrary to what common sense thinks, it's not done through decisionism. "On the other hand, when the judge is required to give reasons for his decisions, he is demanding (much) more than an explanation of the reasons that convinced him (...). This decision will in no way be a 'soliloquy', a 'monologue'".[93]. The movement towards a reasoned decision, arising from responsible authenticity, promotes a legitimate escape from the past, with a view to making the necessary changes in the decision-making process.

In our observation, it seems to us that these two possibilities put forward by Loparic are no longer two possibilities in relation to judges, insofar as, when they choose to exercise this social function in a democratic country (with all the implications we talked about in the first chapter), they give up these two possibilities. The decision of someone who has chosen to exercise the function of deciding in a democratic society can only be to "take charge", otherwise they are not fulfilling their social role, which they themselves have chosen. This is also an ethical issue. Of course you can do things differently, and it's clear that many are doing so, as we see in the decisions. But our question here is more subtle.

This is why we can say, even at the risk of being repetitive: inauthenticity is fatalism, and fatalism is inauthenticity. The role of motivated understanding will be to remove this fatalism, this merely reproductive conduct, but to call Dasein to authenticity, transforming the process of judging into a productive conduct.

It should not be forgotten that, as we saw in chapter one, being-in-the-world is a fundamental existential in the constitution of Dasein, and it, responsibility and authenticity are strongly linked: "'tendentious motivation' is the first step towards the concept that will become central to all of Heidegger's

---

[93] MOTTA, Francisco Jose Borges. *Levando o Direito a Serio: uma critica hermeneutica ao protagonismo judicial*. 2. ed. Porto Alegre: Livraria do Advogado, 2012. p. 138.

work, that of being-in-the-world".[94].

Along these lines, another situation fraught with irresponsibility refers to the decisions of judges who believe that they justify their sentences by issuing a "I accept the ministerial opinion and (in)uphold". Now, both in the "justification" by appropriating mere quotes from jurisprudents - which, in fact, most of the time have no relation between the previous case and the one being analyzed - and in the decision that has all its justification given with a simple reference to a ministerial opinion, without any other consideration, there is an inauthentic judge.

Often, when this judge assumes the inauthentic mode, he commits serious flaws in his judgments, flaws that would certainly not occur if he were in his authentic mode, because in the need to understand the case in order to interpret it, this would become apparent. A serious example of situations like this can be seen in case number 132/1.11.0002510-1, which originated in the district of Sapiranga/RS, in which a debt arising from alimony in a maintenance enforcement action was discussed. The lower court decision, which put an end to the proceedings, was handed down as follows:

> See you. I accept the ministerial request and JUDGE THE DEED EXTINCT, pursuant to article 267, item IV of the Code of Civil Procedure.

In addition to all the problems that decisions like this present, in this particular case the inauthenticity so obscured the meaning of the case that the decision handed down was totally contradictory (in its own terms and with the statements and legal claims of both parties). The appropriation made of the ministerial opinion was already flawed, namely that the ministerial opinion had not understood the parties' statements; therefore, the judge had not unveiled

---

[94] LOPARIC, Zelijko. *On responsibility.* Porto Alegre: EDIPUCRS, 2003. p. 104.

any meaning, causing enormous damage to the jurisdiction. This can best be explained by transcribing excerpts from the judgment that reviewed the decision.

> (...). It is worth noting that the honorable judge in this case, in taking the opinion of the Public Prosecutor's Office as a basis, did not perceive a mismatch between what the creditors and the worthy representative of the Public Prosecutor's Office said.
> "For what it's worth", even if in an extremely summarized way, the creditors in their statement on the defendant's justification definitely did not agree with what was being said by the debtor.
> What was said in the creditors' statement was that, in view of the justification presented by the debtor, they were asking for a judgment and decision on the matter.
> Unfortunately, the Public Prosecutor's Office understood that the creditors were agreeing with what the debtor said in his justification.
> And also, sadly, the sentence extinguished the execution on the basis of what the Public Prosecutor's Office had promoted.
> 3. In fact, there is no agreement.
> On the contrary, graga would be interpretative disagreement (between the parties) about the amount of maintenance in relation to the decision that set the maintenance.
> (...).
> It is worth bearing in mind that it was the same person who made the maintenance order and sentenced the present enforcement.
> Therefore, in the face of the discouraged termination of the case, it is worth relying on an interpretation that, in addition to providing security for the parties, will comply with the constitutional terms of indispensable motivation.
> In view of the above, I accept the preliminary ruling to set aside the judgment [95].

The passage above is self-explanatory and does not require further consideration. The comfort, the tranquillity of the "we" was so present, so strong, in the Magistrate that he possibly didn't even bother to analyze the parties' statements, preferring to resort to a ready-made opinion. If he did, he was wrong again, because he didn't make this clear in his decision and now there's no way of knowing whether or not he analyzed the petitions. What we do know is that he did not decide hermeneutically. It should be noted that the Public Prosecutor's Office, in this case, also had problems analyzing the

---

[95] Civil Appeal No. 70049411044, judged on August 30, 2012, by the Eighth Civil Chamber of the Court of Justice of the State of Rio Grande do Sul. This case has also been analyzed by Streck, in another context.

particular case.

I don't need to say any more about this, but it seems prudent to point out that there are judges who, in order not to oppose the Chamber, out of judicial politics or simple convenience, assume their inauthentic way of being when they say that, although they take the opposite view, for the sake of speed and procedural economy, they follow the rapporteur. This is most often said in oral judgments when the vote is cast (which has already been prepared by the rapporteur [96]).

As a member of a court, the decision-maker is obliged to explain the legal reasons why he agrees or disagrees with the other members responsible for the decision. Nor can it be admitted that "there are cases in which this should be allowed" or that "difficult cases admit judgments of this order". For one thing, just as the mere repetition of decisions is metaphysical, so is the decision in easy or difficult cases.[97](and this is just one more of the theoretical misunderstandings that have taken hold of Brazilian jurists). Is it easier to follow a ready-made vote? There's no doubt about it! Is this hermeneutically and constitutionally legitimate? It seems that the answer is clear.

Likewise, the already established "Block Judgments" in the legal scene, in which the Courts schedule and "judge" dozens of "similar" cases in a single shift on the same day, have a major impact on the Brazilian legal system. This happened with the greatest repercussion in 2007, when the Supreme Court jointly judged more than 4,908 "identical" cases (that is to say, with different parties and even with some causes of action of different origins, but which dealt, in their "equality", with requests for alimony for death). This was a

---

[96] In this sense, Justice Rosa Weber, in her statement on the dosimetry of Hollerbach's sentence in the "Mensalao" case, on October 25, 2012, according to the broadcast of the trial via TV Justiga, stated that she had set the sentence (in the first phase of one of the crimes) at two years. However, "for the sake of the court's agenda", he gave up his convictions (previously expressed and quite different from those of the rapporteur) to follow the rapporteur.

[97] STRECK, Lenio Luiz. Truth and Consensus: Constitution, Hermeneutics and Discursive Theories.

4. ed. Sao Paulo: Saraiva, 2011. p. 358.

paradigmatic case that had some repercussions, perhaps because it was one of the first with so many block judgments, which are now commonplace and even provided for by law (which does not make the decision hermeneutically adequate). However, we should be aware that this happens every day, on a smaller scale, but with the same degree of violation, in state courts all over Brazil and in the Comarcas. To do this, the system is inverted and the party is now obliged to demonstrate, when their case has already been "chosen" to be part of the block, why it doesn't fit into that situation. The right thing to do would be for the judge to justify the similarities between that case and the others so that it can be judged "en bloc".

Another of these potential situations of irresponsible decisions can be found in the use of Sumulas - binding or not - as a way of "substantiating" decisions and closing off interpretations. The Sumulas are an attempt to reduce the complexity of judicial service, trying to put all the possibilities of the world into a simple text. "The problem is that jurists, in establishing limits and concepts, end up hiding them, veiling them. This is because the law 'hates' complexity and likes to simplify. The more you simplify, the more you lose reality. The more complex you can be - which is not the obligation of law - the more you gain in reality".[98]. It's as if it were possible to think that there are ways of limiting the possibilities of projecting oneself, through a text, so that all similar cases can then be decided in a similar way, without too much difficulty.

Certainly, there are jurists who staunchly defend the Sumulas, even calling for more situations to be summarized - "Sumulas are complied with" - in order to guarantee the effectiveness of the Constitution. Some scholars and judges of this trend even auspiciously claim that the Sumulas are a breakthrough and are directly related to the *common law* form of judgment. To

---

[98] HOMMERDING, Adalberto Narciso. Paragraph 3 of Article 515 of the Civil Procedure Code: an analysis in the light of the hermeneutic philosophy (or philosophical hermeneutics) of Heidegger and Gadamer. IN: *Revista da AJURIS/Associaqao dos Juizes do Rio Grande do Sul* - v. 30, n. 91. Porto Alegre: AJURIS, Sep. 2003. p. 39.

demolish this weak argument, it is enough to remember, along with Mauricio Ramires, that summaries are not precedents, precisely because they do not retain the peculiarity of the case (just like the ementions used as grounds for judgments, which in their origin have no relation whatsoever to the situation on which they are based) and lose the DNA that originated them, in favor of an abstraction and generality, which allows them to be applied in almost all cases.[99]that allows them to be applied to almost any situation in which only that original fact is mentioned.

Again, it must be made clear that although the institute of Brazilian Sumulas is highly questionable for a number of reasons, in our current approach, the big problem is how they are used. Once again, "copy and paste" and not justification. If this basic relationship were effectively dealt with, the sumulas could certainly be a good instrument in the face of complexity. However, they currently aren't.

In Streck's words, it seems that it would be possible to "place all the possibilities of application within a legal text. We're still stuck with the 'myth of the given'. Legal metaphysics. Nothing more than that"[100]. In other words, once again jurists and legislators are trying to ignore the overcoming already done by philosophy: separating matters of fact from matters of law; easy cases from difficult cases; interpreting and applying[101]texts with all the possibilities of factual events (summaries).

All these hypotheses represent an attachment to metaphysics; they are splits par excellence between being and being, provided only by metaphysics, remembering that belief in metaphysics puts the judge on the road to

[99] RAMIRES, Mauricio. *Criticism of the application of precedents in Brazilian law*. Porto Alegre: Livraria do Advogado, 2010. p. 61.

[100] STRECK, Lenio Luiz. By way of preface: a libel against the *habitus dogmaticus*. IN: *RAMIRES, Mauricio. Critique of the application of precedents in Brazilian law*. Porto Alegre: Livraria do Advogado, 2010.

[101] STRECK, Lenio Luiz. *What is this - I decide according to my conscience?* Vol. I. Porto Alegre: Livraria do Advogado, 2010. p. 36.

inauthenticity and irresponsibility. The more one tries to formulate assertoric statements with the pretension of predicting (and totally limiting) the future, the more one hides the meaning of what one is judging. That's because language doesn't cover everything. There's always something left over. That's why we have to admit that we can't say everything. Something will always be left out. As law is essentially language, it must be admitted that the understanding of law will always be hermeneutic, because if language places us in the world, we will always have our pre-understanding, since we are inserted within a translation. Since the understanding of law is hermeneutic and, therefore, hermeneutic and self-understanding, we can say that we are inside a circle where we can see that being is always being of an entity. If it is always a being of a being, then it is not separate, because being differs from being only ontologically, but not ontically. And it will always be a "being-in", because it cannot conceive, for example, of a text or a law "loose in the air" waiting for a "docking".[102].

Hermeneutically, it can be said that

> The binding summula is a metacondition of meaning, producing a monologic discourse and preventing the necessary hermeneutic alterity. In this way, the problem with summaries does not lie in the fact that they are correct or incorrect, but in the function that this mechanism plays in the legal system and its consequences for access to justice and the quality of the decisions to be made by judges and courts.[103].

As has already been said, if the judges are not authentic, the cases will not be unveiled. Without unveiling, there is no understanding, and without understanding, there is no way that an adequate decision can be made to the point of producing meaning and communicating with society, to which one is entitled at any level of jurisdiction.

> That is why, when the judge decides using, for example, "settled case law", he is not the one who is deciding, in other words, he is not the one who is responsible. In the same way, if he doesn't decide the merits, he has no responsibility for the judgment of the case, even if the issue is

---

[102] HOMMERDING, Adalberto Narciso. Paragraph 3 of Article 515 of the Civil Procedure Code: an analysis in the light of the hermeneutic philosophy (or philosophical hermeneutics) of Heidegger and Gadamer. IN: *Revista da AJURIS/Associaqao dos Juizes do Rio Grande do Sul* - v. 30, n. 91. Porto Alegre: AJURIS, Sep. 2003. p. 46.

[103] STRECK, Lenio Luiz; ABBOUD, Georges. What *is this - judicial precedent and binding sumulas?* Porto Alegre: Livraria do Advogado, 2013. p. 120.

one of law, because this also requires interpretation [104].

And in Brazil, there seems to be an acquiescence on the part of jurists, and especially the doctrine, to all these situations that have been described above. What's more, in some cases, there is even an agreement that this is the case. "When someone conforms, therefore, to something finished, they are, in fact, 'covering up' the thing"[105]. That's why the judge needs to be authentic and analyze each case carefully, giving reasons for the case and explaining the meaning of his arguments. Thus, hermeneutics is the tool that allows the decision-maker to be authentic when anguish calls. This is because philosophical hermeneutics is critical, and being critical, it becomes productive.

When the judge, man (Dasein), is inauthentic, he "breaks", "blocks" the possibility of Being, which is his essence, which constitutes apao. And man is essentially being-power. "Common sense is unaware of the fact that it can only really know what is and what is being, even if it hasn't grasped it conceptually. Common sense misunderstands understanding. The movement of inquiry into being is a circular movement and is therefore finite. To break this circle of finitude by elements intrinsic to the questioning of the meaning of being is to go against the fundamental structures of being-there".[106]. As has already been said, the question can only be asked in the authentic way of being. Hermeneutically, authenticity is the key to more qualified and committed judicial decisions.

---

[104] HOMMERDING, Adalberto Narciso. Paragraph 3 of Article 515 of the Civil Procedure Code: an analysis in the light of the hermeneutic philosophy (or philosophical hermeneutics) of Heidegger and Gadamer. IN: *Revista da AJURIS/Associaqao dos Juizes do Rio Grande do Sul - v. 30, n. 91. Porto Alegre: AJURIS, Sep. 2003. p.20.

[105] HOMMERDING, Adalberto Narciso. Paragraph 3 of Article 515 of the Civil Procedure Code: an analysis in the light of the hermeneutic philosophy (or philosophical hermeneutics) of Heidegger and Gadamer. IN: *Revista da AJURIS/Associaqao dos Juizes do Rio Grande do Sul* - v. 30, n. 91. Porto Alegre: AJURIS, Sep. 2003. p. 26.

[106] HOMMERDING, Adalberto Narciso. Paragraph 3 of Article 515 of the Civil Procedure Code: an analysis in the light of the hermeneutic philosophy (or philosophical hermeneutics) of Heidegger and Gadamer. IN: *Revista da AJURIS/Associaqao dos Juizes do Rio Grande do Sul* - v. 30, n. 91. Porto Alegre: AJURIS, Sep. 2003. p. 34.

Final considerations

Throughout this book we have shown how the inauthentic way of being can undermine the hermeneutic responsibility of judges, negatively affecting the delivery of justice. It is hoped that this has been explained in such a way that a correct understanding of the text has been extracted. If not, in this final space, some more considerations will be made along these lines.

In three chapters, we tried to answer the questions raised at the start of the debate. In the first part, we looked at the extraordinary relevance of Martin Heidegger's work Sein und Zeit (Being and Time) for society as a whole, especially for law, which works with understanding and interpretation. This is where the first important observation emerged: law is not immune to the changes brought about by philosophy. The mere fact that it exists already means that it is linked to philosophy. Law works with texts and produces texts. When we disregard the changes brought about by Heidegger, starting with Being and Time, we end up not allowing texts to say what they have to say. Therefore, we need to stop trying to give words the meaning we want - in isolation - and dedicate ourselves to effectively understanding their meaning in communication.

In section two, the concern was to discuss the modes of being of authentic and inauthentic Dasein, as well as the possibilities of responsibility or irresponsibility arising from each mode of being. By using these concepts coined by Heidegger, it was possible to point out the damage suffered by law and society in the face of the inauthentic experience of a judge. The effort was also directed at showing how classical metaphysics, which has long since been overcome by philosophy, still permeates law and prevents certain meanings from being revealed and communicated.

Finally, the last chapter showed how philosophical hermeneutics based on Heidegger is a qualified way of observing judicial decision-making. In this chapter, we were able to compare real decisions with all the arguments we had previously constructed. As a result, it became clear that, for the most part, judges do not assume their authentic way of being when making decisions, but merely repeat, copy and delegate their functional obligation. As we have seen, this affects democracy and social communication as a whole, not just in relation to those involved in the process. Such behavior needs to be analyzed and criticized by Brazilian doctrine in a swift and forceful manner.

Thus, these three points illuminate the path as a means of structuring an observation based on Being, linked to understanding and language. Authenticity and inauthenticity are essential to understanding. Therefore, a correct understanding of the case they are judging will only come about once the decision-makers adopt their authentic way of being. There is no possibility of thinking or providing adequate answers in inauthenticity. This is because, in inauthenticity, decisions or choices are only possible for everyday issues, automatic issues - brushing your teeth, driving - but a judicial decision, even for a judge, cannot be considered an everyday thing. Authenticity is therefore the condition of possibility for a responsible response. In authenticity we can understand the world in a richer way, with its full participation in the public context. Authenticity opens up spaces for new meanings arising from the singularity of Dasein.

In this way, what needs to be clarified is that we understand, from this theoretical perspective, unlike other researchers, that it is not possible to think of a single correct answer, and much less is it possible to predict or limit judicial decisions. On the contrary, as each Dasein has its own singularity, and as each one can live in both authenticity and inauthenticity, this indicates that the answers will have to be varied among the judges. As the authentic way of being opens up space for new meanings arising from singularity, these meanings that contemplate participation in the public context can be different. And that's not a problem, as long as the judge expressly states why he or she made that decision, in the terms we discuss in this book. This impossibility of a single correct answer is a realization of possibilities. Remember: to understand is to project oneself, and the possibilities of projecting oneself are infinite. Therefore, a theory that claims that, based on this theoretical framework, it is possible to think of a limitation of judicial responses for each case under discussion makes no sense, nor does a theory that aims to achieve certainty with regard to the best or worst ways of deciding. Hermeneutics deals with ontological understanding, and that tells us a lot.

That is why, although inauthenticity is a way of being of Dasein, like the others, it cannot be tolerated that a judge remains in this comfort when making a decision. A judge can be inauthentic and blindly - or consciously - follow "us", "the others" in his personal choices, precisely because they only affect him and the people who are connected to him by will. However, when the decision is made to pursue a career in which the primary function is decision-making, Dasein cannot allow itself to decide as others do, just for the sake of convenience. Convenience is tempting, it seduces, because it removes hermeneutic responsibilities, but it prevents the meaning of something, as something, from being revealed. In other words, it will prevent the peculiarities of that case from being revealed, corrupting judicial service and undermining democracy. And therefore all citizens.

But what is the difference between an authentic decision and an inauthentic one? What's wrong with the decision-maker being inauthentic? It seems worth repeating: the judge, in taking on the social commitment of being a decision-maker in the law - with decisions that affect the dynamics of the whole of society - also takes on the commitment of understanding the cases he or she will judge. The judge's own understanding depends on his authentic way of being in order to be fully realized. Now, if man is the only being capable of understanding with any rationality, he has an obligation to commit himself to this understanding, so that he can interpret and then judge.

Deciding in inauthenticity is a return to classical metaphysics.

It should be noted that our primary concern, when observing from the hermeneutic path, is not linked to legality - a "copied" decision, an inauthentic decision can still be legal and legally legitimate - but to the way of Being. If the way of Being is our basis, we cannot think or predict the best ways of acting or, in this case, deciding. We find this view in other authors, including, at times, those quoted in our text.

For us, regardless of the matrix we adopt, be it Luhmannian or hermeneutic, we maintain our observation that we have no way of foreseeing the content of the decision; in fact, we don't even want to. This is definitely not a problem. On the contrary, it opens up good possibilities for different and appropriate responses. In this book, we have just shown that, even through hermeneutics, this observation is possible.

In a final word: at this time in history, when we are still fighting to enforce democracy, it is necessary for someone who is willing to be a judge to allow themselves to feel anguish and heed the silent call of their conscience to take upon themselves their Being, assuming themselves to be an authentic Judge.

References

Civil Appeal No. 70049411044, judged on August 30, 2012, by the Eighth Civil Chamber of the Court of Justice of the State of Rio Grande do Sul.

Criminal Appeal No. 70012342515, judged on January 25, 2006, by the Fifth Criminal Chamber of the Court of Justice of the State of Rio Grande do Sul.

DREYFUS, Hubert L. *Being-in-the-World: a commentary on Heidegger's Being and Time, Division I.* Cambridge, Massachusetts/London/ England: The MIT Press, 1991.

DWORKIN, Ronald. *A question of principle.* 2.ed. Sao Paulo: Matirns Fontes, 2003.

ENGELMANN, Wilson. *Natural Law, Ethics and Hermeneutics.* Porto Alegre: Livraria do Advogado, 2007.

GADAMER, Hans-Georg. Truth and Method I: *fundamental traces of a philosophical hermeneutics.* Translated by Flavio Paulo Meurer and Enio Paulo Giachini. 11.ed. Braganga Paulista: Editora Universitaria Sao Francisco; Petropolis: Editora Vozes, 2011.

. *Truth and Method II: complements and index.* Translated by Enio Paulo Gaichini 2. ed. Braganga Paulista: Editora Universitaria Sao Francisco; Petropolis: Editora Vozes, 2004.

GUIGNON, Charles. *Authenticity, moral values and psychotherapy.* IN: The Cambridge Companion To Heidegger. New York: Cambridge University Press, 1993.

HAAR, Michel. *Heidegger and the essence of man.* Translated by Ana Cristina Alves. Lisbon: Instituto Piaget. 1997.

HEIDEGGER, Martin. *Conferences and philosophical writings.* Translated by Vergilio Ferreira. São Paulo: Victor Civita, 1973 (The Thinkers, XLV).

. *Introduction to Philosophy.* Translated by Marco Antonio Casanova. Sao Paulo: Martins Fontes, 2009.

. *Sein Un Zeit.* Tubingen: Max Niemeyer Verlag, 2006.

. *Zollikon Seminars: protocols, dialogues, letters.*
Translated by Gabriella Arnhold and Maria de Fatima de Almeida Prado. 2.ed.
Braganga Paulista: Editora Universitaria Sao Francisco; Petropolis: Editora
Vozes, 2009.

. *Being and Time.* Translated by Jorge Eduardo Rivera C. Santiago del Chile:
Editorial Universitaria, S.A., 1997.

HESSE, Johannes. *Theory of Knowledge.* Sao Paulo: Martins Fontes, 2000.

HOMMERDING, Adalberto Narciso. Paragraph 3 of Article 515 of the Civil
Procedure Code: an analysis in the light of the hermeneutic philosophy (or
philosophical hermeneutics) of Heidegger and Gadamer. IN: *Revista da
AJURIS/Associagao dos Jufzes do Rio Grande do Sul* - v. 30, n. 91. Porto
Alegre: AJURIS, Sep. 2003. p. 9-57.

HUSSERL, Edmund. *Logical Investigations: Sixth Investigation: Elements of a
Phenomenological Elucidation of Knowledge.* Translated by Ziljko Loparic and
Andrea Maria Altino de Campos Loparic. Sao Paulo: Nova Cultural, 1998
(The Thinkers).

LIMA, Vinicius de Melo. *Teoria Hermeneutica da Responsabilidade Decisoria:
Direitos Sociais entre Ativismo Judicial e Decisao Jurldica Democratica.*
Curitiba: Jurua Editora. 2016.

LOPARIC, Zelijko. *On responsibility.* Porto Alegre: EDIPUCRS, 2003.

LUIZ, Fernando Vieira. *Judicial Decision Theory: from Ricardo Lorenzetti's
paradigms to Lenio Streck's adequate response to the Constitution.* Porto
Alegre: Livraria do Advogado, 2011.

MORA, Jose Ferrater. Metaphysics. IN: *Dicionario de Filosofia.* Sao Paulo:
Martins Fontes, 1988. p. 467.

MOTTA, Francisco Jose Borges. *Levando o Direito a Serio: uma crticica
hermeneutica ao protagonismo judicial.* 2. ed. Porto Alegre: Livraria do
Advogado, 2012.

OLIVEIRA, RAFAEL Tomaz de. *Decisao Judicial e o conceito* de *princípio: a
hermeneutica e a (in) determinação do Direito.* Porto Alegre: Livraria do
Advogado, 2008.

PASQUA, Herve. *Introduction to Martin Heidegger's Being and Time.*
Translated by Joana Chaves. Lisbon: Instituto Piaget, 1995.

RAMIRES, Mauricio. *Criticism of the application of precedents in Brazilian law.* Porto Alegre: Livraria do Advogado, 2010.

REALE, Giovani; ANTISERI, Dario. *History of Philosophy: From Romanticism to the present day.* Vol. 3. Sao Paulo: Paulus, 1991. p, 581-82.

RESWEBER, Jean-Paul. *The thought of Martin Hiedegger.* Translated by Joao Agostinho A. Santos. Coimbra: Livraria Almedina, 1979.

SAFRANSKI, RUDIGER. *Heidegger: a German master between good and evil.* Translated by Lya Lett Luft. Sao Paulo: Geragao Editorial, 2005.

SARTRE, Jean-Paul. *Being and Nothingness: An Essay in Phenomenological Ontology.* Translated by Paulo Perdigao. 5. ed. Petropolis: Vozes, 1997.

STEIN, Ernildo. *Introduction to the thought of Martin Heidegger.* Porto Alegre: EDIPUCRS, 2002.

. *Thinking and making mistakes: an adjustment with Heidegger.* ijuf: Editora UNUJUI, 2011.

. *Six studies on "Being and Time".* 4.ed. Petropolis: Editora Vozes, 2008.

STRECK, Lenio Luiz. By way of preface: a libel against the *habitus dogmaticus.* IN: *RAMIRES, Mauricio. Critique of the application of precedents in Brazilian law.* Porto Alegre: Livraria do Advogado, 2010.

. Heidegger, Martin, 1889-1976. IN: BARRETTO, Vicente de Paulo (Org.), *Dicionario* de *Filosofia do Direito.* Sao Leopoldo: Editora Unisinos; Rio de Janeiro/RJ: Livraria Editora Renovar, 2009. p. 426-27.

. Hermeneutica Juridica e(m) Crise: uma exploragao hermeneutica da construgao do Direito. 8. ed. Porto Alegre: Livraria do Advogado, 2009.

. *What is this - I decide according to my conscience?* Vol. I. Porto Alegre: Livraria do Advogado, 2010.

. *Truth and Consensus: Constitution, Hermeneutics and Discursive Theories.* 4.ed. Sao Paulo: Saraiva, 2011.

; ABBOUD, Georges. What is this - judicial precedent and binding precedents? Porto Alegre: Livraria do Advogado, 2012.

TASSINARI, Clarissa. *Jurisdiction and Judicial Activism: the limits of judicial action.* Porto Alegre: Livraria do Advogado, 2013.

TUGENDHAT, Ernest. *Autoconciencia y Autodeterminacion: uma interpretation linguistico-analitica.* Madrid: FCE, 1993.

WEBB, David. *Heidegger, Ethics and the Practice of Ontology.* London/New York: Continuum Studies in Continental Philosophy, 2009.

WEBBER, Marcos Andre. *Ethics and Existence: a Heideggerian contribution.* Caxias do Sul: EDUCS, 2016.

WEBBER, Suelen. *Decision, Risk and Health: the paradox of judicial decision in the face of requests for experimental medicines.* Curitiba: Jurua, 2013.

WEBBER, Suelen. *Observations on the Person Form and its Reflections on the System of Law and Politics.* In press, to be published in the next volume of Cadernos da Anpof.

WILLIAM, J. Richardson. Humanism and Existential Psychology. IN: GREENING, Thomas C. (Org.) *Existential-Humanist Psychology.* Translated by Eduardo de Almeida. Rio de Janeiro: Zahar Editores, 1975, p. 177-78.

WITTGENSTEIN. Ludwing. *Logico-Philosophical Treatise; Philosophical Investigations.* Translated by M. S. Lourengo. 3.ed. Lisbon: Calouste Gulbenkian Foundation, 2002.

yes
I want morebooks!

Buy your books fast and straightforward online - at one of world's fastest growing online book stores! Environmentally sound due to Print-on-Demand technologies.

Buy your books online at
www.morebooks.shop

Kaufen Sie Ihre Bücher schnell und unkompliziert online – auf einer der am schnellsten wachsenden Buchhandelsplattformen weltweit! Dank Print-On-Demand umwelt- und ressourcenschonend produziert.

Bücher schneller online kaufen
www.morebooks.shop

info@omniscriptum.com
www.omniscriptum.com

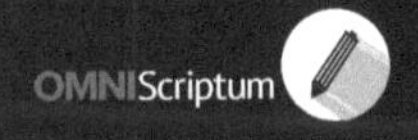